# WILLIAM SHAKESPEARE
# MACBETH

Illustrated by Von

RAVETTE BOOKS LIMITED

Published by Ravette Books Limited,
25-31 Tavistock Place, London WC1H 9SU

ISBN  185304 652 3

Edited by Anne Tauté
Lettering by Elitta Fell, Westerham, Kent
Origination by Colourscan Co Pte Ltd, Singapore
Printed by BPC Paulton Books,  Bristol

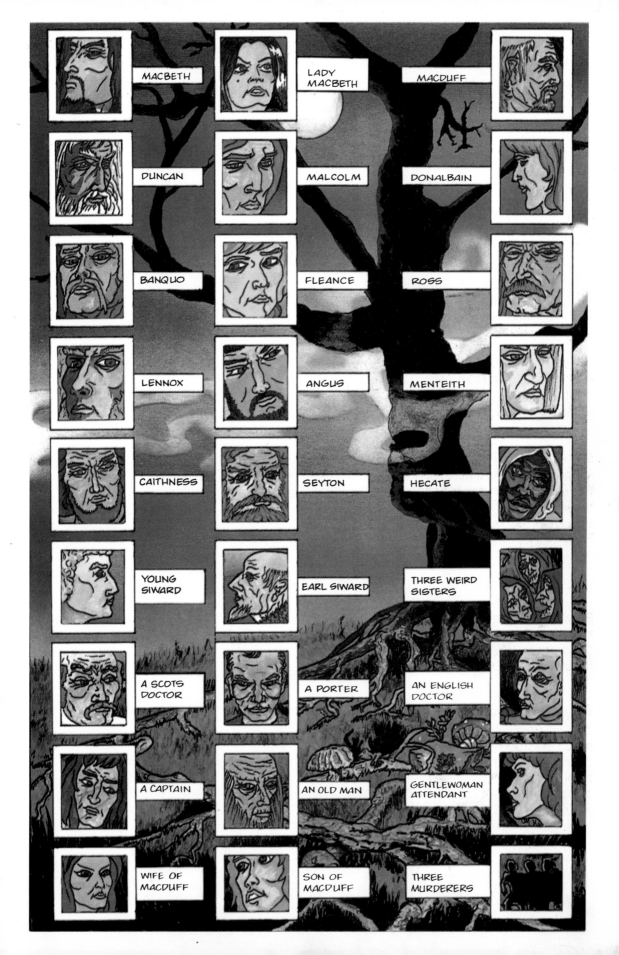

# THE PLOT

**Macbeth** and **Banquo**, generals of **King Duncan's** army, have defeated a rebellion and repulsed a Norwegian invasion. Going home they are stopped by three witches who tell Macbeth he will be thane of Cawdor and King of Scotland. But Banquo's children will be future kings. As they vanish in the mist, the first prophecy comes true. Inspired by their words Macbeth considers murder. **Lady Macbeth** sharpens his resolve, and he stabs Duncan to death.

The crown is now his, but fear and suspicion shadow him. Macbeth cannot forget the prediction made to Banquo. He hires assassins to kill his friend, but Banquo's dreadful ghost comes back to haunt him. Macbeth seeks out the witches and is warned against **Macduff**, the thane of Fife, but told no harm can come to him till someone not 'of woman born' appears, and Birnam wood moves.

Macbeth is told Macduff has fled to England to join forces with **Malcolm**, the son of murdered Duncan. Enraged he has Macduff's wife and family slaughtered. Lady Macbeth demented by so much bloodshed, starts sleepwalking.

Macbeth prepares to defend his fortress and is shaken to hear that Birnam wood is moving. Hidden by branches hacked from the forest Malcolm and Macduff's army overruns the castle. Macbeth resists attack, confident no man can kill him. But Macduff reveals he was cut from the womb and so not 'born' of woman. They fight. Macbeth is slain. Malcolm is at last made King.

Written in 1606, on the wave of support and loyalty to King James **VI** & **I** after the Gunpowder Plot attempt on his life, Shakespeare was deliberately indulging his monarch's known obsessions with Scottish history, ancestry, and witchcraft. Murder, treason,suspicion,witches,were the topics of the day,and public interest was particularly caught by the case of a priest who, having been accused of lying at his trial, maintained that he was not lying, but merely concealing the truth with double meaning . . .

ACT I, SCENE I

WHEN SHALL WE THREE MEET AGAIN?
IN THUNDER, LIGHTNING, OR IN RAIN?

WHEN THE HURLY-BURLY'S DONE,
WHEN THE BATTLE'S LOST AND WON.

THAT WILL BE ERE THE SET OF SUN.

WHERE THE PLACE?

UPON THE HEATH.

THERE TO MEET WITH MACBETH.

I COME, GREY-MALKIN!

PADDOCK CALLS.

ANON!

FAIR IS FOUL,
AND FOUL IS FAIR:
HOVER THROUGH THE FOG
AND FILTHY AIR.

1

WHAT BLOODY MAN IS THAT?
HE CAN REPORT, AS SEEMETH BY HIS PLIGHT,
OF THE REVOLT THE NEWEST STATE.

THIS IS THE SERGEANT, WHO
LIKE A GOOD AND HARDY SOLDIER
FOUGHT 'GAINST MY CAPTIVITY.
HAIL, BRAVE FRIEND! SAY TO THE KING
THE KNOWLEDGE OF THE BROIL
AS THOU DIDST LEAVE IT.

DOUBTFUL IT STOOD,
AS TWO SPENT SWIMMERS,
THAT DO CLING TOGETHER
AND CHOKE THEIR ART.
THE MERCILESS
MACDONWALD—
WORTHY TO BE A REBEL,
FOR TO THAT THE
MULTIPLYING VILLAINIES
OF NATURE DO SWARM
UPON HIM—

FROM THE WESTERN ISLES
OF KERNS AND GALLOWGLASSES IS SUPPLIED;
AND FORTUNE, ON HIS DAMNÈD QUARREL
SMILING, SHOWED LIKE A REBEL'S WHORE:
BUT ALL'S TOO WEAK:

FOR BRAVE MACBETH - WELL HE DESERVES THAT NAME -
DISDAINING FORTUNE, WITH HIS BRANDISHED STEEL,
WHICH SMOKED WITH BLOODY EXECUTION,
LIKE VALOUR'S MINION CARVED OUT HIS PASSAGE,

TILL HE FACED
THE SLAVE;
WHICH NE'ER SHOOK HANDS,
NOR BADE FAREWELL
TO HIM,

TILL HE UNSEAMED HIM
FROM THE NAVE TO THE
CHOPS, AND FIXED HIS
HEAD UPON OUR BATTLEMENTS.

GOD SAVE THE KING!

WHENCE CAM'ST THOU, WORTHY THANE?

FROM FIFE, GREAT KING.

WHERE THE NORWEYAN BANNERS FLOUT THE SKY AND FAN OUR PEOPLE COLD.

NORWAY HIMSELF, WITH TERRIBLE NUMBERS, ASSISTED BY THAT MOST DISLOYAL TRAITOR, THE THANE OF CAWDOR, BEGAN A DISMAL CONFLICT;

TILL THAT BELLONA'S BRIDEGROOM, LAPPED IN PROOF, CONFRONTED HIM WITH SELF-COMPARISONS,

POINT AGAINST POINT, REBELLIOUS ARM 'GAINST ARM, CURBING HIS LAVISH SPIRIT: AND TO CONCLUDE, THE VICTORY FELL ON US.

GREAT HAPPINESS!

THAT NOW SWENO, THE NORWAYS' KING, CRAVES COMPOSITION; NOR WOULD WE DEIGN HIM BURIAL OF HIS MEN TILL HE DISBURSÈD, AT SAINT COLME'S INCH, TEN THOUSAND DOLLARS TO OUR GENERAL USE.

NO MORE THAT THANE OF CAWDOR SHALL DECEIVE OUR BOSOM INTEREST. GO PRONOUNCE HIS PRESENT DEATH, AND WITH HIS FORMER TITLE, GREET MACBETH.

I'LL SEE IT DONE.

WHAT HE HATH LOST, NOBLE MACBETH HATH WON.

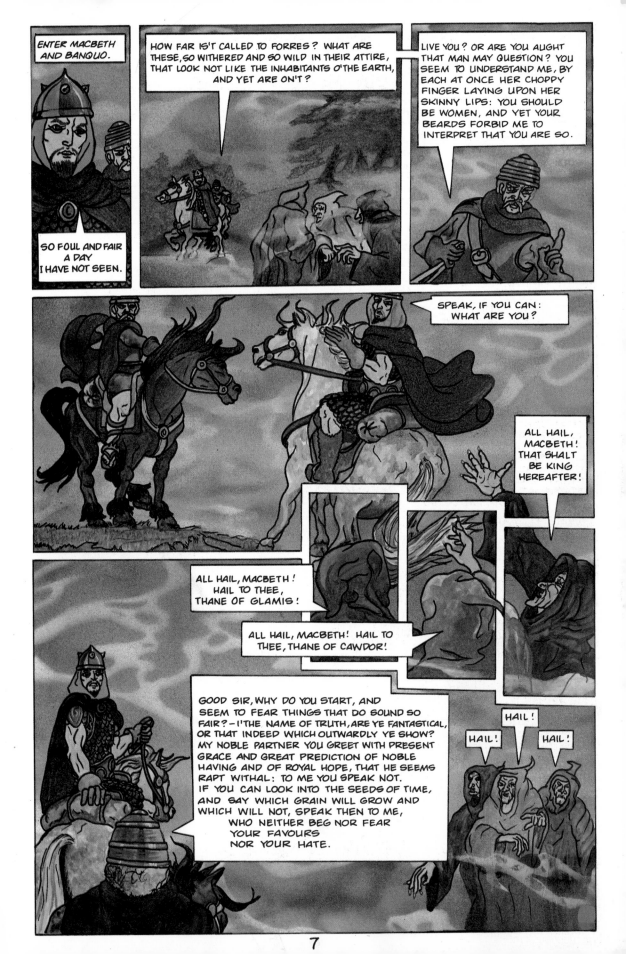

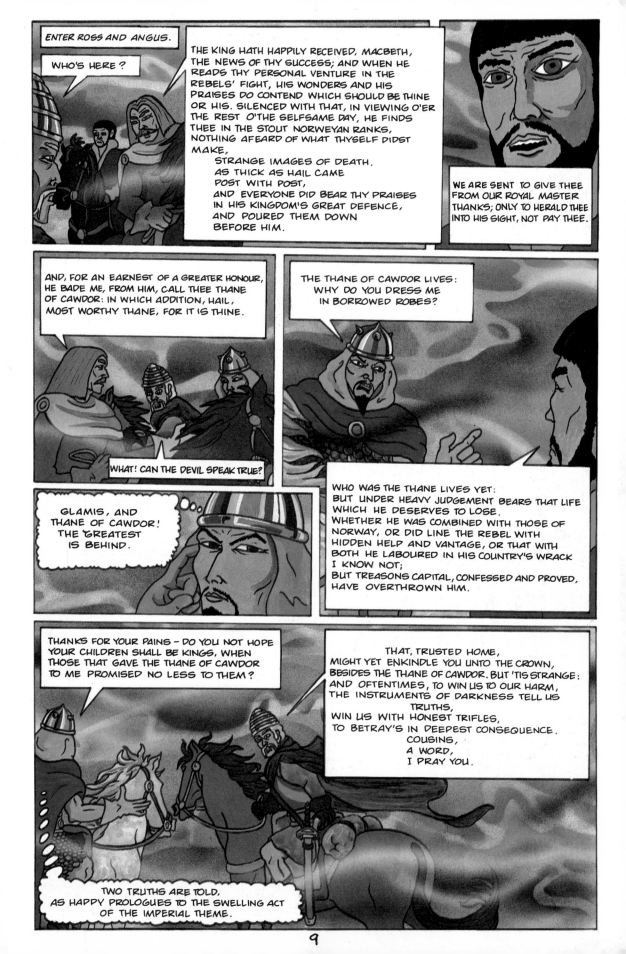

ENTER ROSS AND ANGUS.

WHO'S HERE?

THE KING HATH HAPPILY RECEIVED, MACBETH, THE NEWS OF THY SUCCESS; AND WHEN HE READS THY PERSONAL VENTURE IN THE REBELS' FIGHT, HIS WONDERS AND HIS PRAISES DO CONTEND WHICH SHOULD BE THINE OR HIS. SILENCED WITH THAT, IN VIEWING O'ER THE REST O'THE SELFSAME DAY, HE FINDS THEE IN THE STOUT NORWEYAN RANKS, NOTHING AFEARD OF WHAT THYSELF DIDST MAKE,
STRANGE IMAGES OF DEATH.
AS THICK AS HAIL CAME
POST WITH POST,
AND EVERYONE DID BEAR THY PRAISES
IN HIS KINGDOM'S GREAT DEFENCE,
AND POURED THEM DOWN
BEFORE HIM.

WE ARE SENT TO GIVE THEE FROM OUR ROYAL MASTER THANKS; ONLY TO HERALD THEE INTO HIS SIGHT, NOT PAY THEE.

AND, FOR AN EARNEST OF A GREATER HONOUR, HE BADE ME, FROM HIM, CALL THEE THANE OF CAWDOR: IN WHICH ADDITION, HAIL, MOST WORTHY THANE, FOR IT IS THINE.

WHAT! CAN THE DEVIL SPEAK TRUE?

THE THANE OF CAWDOR LIVES:
WHY DO YOU DRESS ME
IN BORROWED ROBES?

WHO WAS THE THANE LIVES YET:
BUT UNDER HEAVY JUDGEMENT BEARS THAT LIFE WHICH HE DESERVES TO LOSE.
WHETHER HE WAS COMBINED WITH THOSE OF NORWAY, OR DID LINE THE REBEL WITH HIDDEN HELP AND VANTAGE, OR THAT WITH BOTH HE LABOURED IN HIS COUNTRY'S WRACK I KNOW NOT;
BUT TREASONS CAPITAL, CONFESSED AND PROVED, HAVE OVERTHROWN HIM.

GLAMIS, AND THANE OF CAWDOR! THE 'GREATEST IS BEHIND.

THANKS FOR YOUR PAINS – DO YOU NOT HOPE YOUR CHILDREN SHALL BE KINGS, WHEN THOSE THAT GAVE THE THANE OF CAWDOR TO ME PROMISED NO LESS TO THEM?

THAT, TRUSTED HOME,
MIGHT YET ENKINDLE YOU UNTO THE CROWN, BESIDES THE THANE OF CAWDOR. BUT 'TIS STRANGE: AND OFTENTIMES, TO WIN US TO OUR HARM, THE INSTRUMENTS OF DARKNESS TELL US
TRUTHS,
WIN US WITH HONEST TRIFLES,
TO BETRAY'S IN DEEPEST CONSEQUENCE.
COUSINS,
A WORD,
I PRAY YOU.

TWO TRUTHS ARE TOLD,
AS HAPPY PROLOGUES TO THE SWELLING ACT OF THE IMPERIAL THEME.

IS EXECUTION DONE ON CAWDOR? ARE NOT THOSE IN COMMISSION YET RETURNED?

MY LIEGE, THEY ARE NOT YET COME BACK. BUT I HAVE SPOKE WITH ONE THAT SAW HIM DIE; WHO DID REPORT THAT VERY FRANKLY HE CONFESSED HIS TREASONS, IMPLORED YOUR HIGHNESS' PARDON, AND SET FORTH A DEEP REPENTANCE. NOTHING IN HIS LIFE BECAME HIM LIKE THE LEAVING IT;

HE DIED AS ONE THAT HAD BEEN STUDIED IN HIS DEATH TO THROW AWAY THE DEAREST THING HE OWED, AS 'TWERE A CARELESS TRIFLE.

ENTER MACBETH, BANQUO, ROSS AND ANGUS.

THERE'S NO ART TO FIND THE MIND'S CONSTRUCTION IN THE FACE: HE WAS A GENTLEMAN ON WHOM I BUILT AN ABSOLUTE TRUST.

O WORTHIEST COUSIN!

THE SIN OF MY INGRATITUDE EVEN NOW WAS HEAVY ON ME. THOU ART SO FAR BEFORE, THAT SWIFTEST WING OF RECOMPENSE IS SLOW TO OVERTAKE THEE. WOULD THOU HADST LESS DESERVED, THAT THE PROPORTION BOTH OF THANKS AND PAYMENT MIGHT HAVE BEEN MINE! ONLY I HAVE LEFT TO SAY, MORE IS THY DUE THAN MORE THAN ALL CAN PAY.

THE SERVICE AND THE LOYALTY I OWE, IN DOING IT, PAYS ITSELF. YOUR HIGHNESS' PART IS TO RECEIVE OUR DUTIES: AND OUR DUTIES ARE TO YOUR THRONE AND STATE, CHILDREN AND SERVANTS; WHICH DO BUT WHAT THEY SHOULD, BY DOING EVERYTHING SAFE TOWARD YOUR LOVE AND HONOUR.

WELCOME HITHER: I HAVE BEGUN TO PLANT THEE, AND WILL LABOUR TO MAKE THEE FULL OF GROWING. NOBLE BANQUO, THAT HAST NO LESS DESERVED, NOR MUST BE KNOWN NO LESS TO HAVE DONE SO, LET ME ENFOLD THEE AND HOLD THEE TO MY HEART.

THERE IF I GROW, THE HARVEST IS YOUR OWN.

MY PLENTEOUS JOYS, WANTON IN FULLNESS, SEEK TO HIDE THEMSELVES IN DROPS OF SORROW. SONS, KINSMEN, THANES, AND YOU WHOSE PLACES ARE THE NEAREST, KNOW WE WILL ESTABLISH OUR ESTATE UPON OUR ELDEST, MALCOLM, WHOM WE NAME HEREAFTER THE PRINCE OF CUMBERLAND: WHICH HONOUR MUST NOT UNACCOMPANIED INVEST HIM ONLY, BUT SIGNS OF NOBLENESS, LIKE STARS, SHALL SHINE ON ALL DESERVERS.

They met me in the day of success; and I have learned by the perfectest report, they have more in them than mortal knowledge.

When I burned in desire to question them further, they made themselves air, into which they vanished. Whiles I stood rapt in the wonder of it, came missives from the king, who all-hailed me 'Thane of Cawdor'; by which title before, these weird sisters saluted me, and referred me to the coming on of time, with 'Hail King that shalt be!' This have I thought good to deliver thee, my dearest partner of greatness, that thou mightest not lose the dues of rejoicing by being ignorant of what greatness is promised thee.

Lay it to thy heart, and farewell.

*Macbeth*

GLAMIS THOU ART, AND CAWDOR,
AND SHALT BE WHAT THOU ART PROMISED.
YET DO I FEAR THY NATURE: IT IS TOO FULL O'THE
MILK OF HUMAN KINDNESS TO CATCH THE NEAREST
WAY. THOU WOULDST BE GREAT, ART NOT
WITHOUT AMBITION, BUT WITHOUT THE ILLNESS
SHOULD ATTEND IT. WHAT THOU WOULDST HIGHLY,
THAT WOULDST THOU HOLILY; WOULDST NOT
PLAY FALSE, AND YET WOULDST WRONGLY WIN.
THOU'DST HAVE, GREAT GLAMIS, THAT WHICH
CRIES, 'THUS THOU MUST DO' IF THOU HAVE IT,
AND THAT WHICH RATHER THOU DOST FEAR
TO DO THAN WISHEST SHOULD BE UNDONE.
HIE THEE HITHER,

14

ACT 1, SCENE VI

THIS CASTLE HAS A PLEASANT SEAT; THE AIR NIMBLY AND SWEETLY RECOMMENDS ITSELF UNTO OUR GENTLE SENSES.

THIS GUEST OF SUMMER, THE TEMPLE-HAUNTING MARTLET, DOES APPROVE BY HIS LOVED MANSIONRY THAT THE HEAVEN'S BREATH SMELLS WOOINGLY HERE.

NO JUTTY, FRIEZE, BUTTRESS, NOR COIGN OF VANTAGE, BUT THIS BIRD HATH MADE HIS PENDENT BED AND PROCREANT CRADLE: WHERE THEY MOST BREED AND HAUNT, I HAVE OBSERVED THE AIR IS DELICATE.

SEE, SEE, OUR HONOURED HOSTESS! THE LOVE THAT FOLLOWS US SOMETIME IS OUR TROUBLE, WHICH STILL WE THANK AS LOVE. HEREIN I TEACH YOU HOW YOU SHALL BID GOD 'IELD US FOR YOUR PAINS, AND THANK US FOR YOUR TROUBLE.

ALL OUR SERVICE IN EVERY POINT TWICE DONE, AND THEN DONE DOUBLE, WERE POOR AND SINGLE BUSINESS TO CONTEND AGAINST THOSE HONOURS DEEP AND BROAD.

WHEREWITH YOUR MAJESTY LOADS OUR HOUSE: FOR THOSE OF OLD, AND THE LATE DIGNITIES HEAPED UP TO THEM, WE REST YOUR HERMITS.

WHERE'S THE THANE OF CAWDOR? WE COURSED HIM AT THE HEELS AND HAD A PURPOSE TO BE HIS PURVEYOR: BUT HE RIDES WELL, AND HIS GREAT LOVE, SHARP AS HIS SPUR, HATH HOLP HIM TO HIS HOME BEFORE US. FAIR AND NOBLE HOSTESS, WE ARE YOUR GUEST TONIGHT.

GIVE ME YOUR HAND: CONDUCT ME TO MINE HOST. WE LOVE HIM HIGHLY, AND SHALL CONTINUE OUR GRACES TOWARDS HIM.

BY YOUR LEAVE, HOSTESS.

YOUR SERVANTS EVER HAVE THEIRS, THEMSELVES, AND WHAT IS THEIRS, IN COMPT, TO MAKE THEIR AUDIT AT YOUR HIGHNESS' PLEASURE, STILL TO RETURN YOUR OWN.

ENTER LADY MACBETH.

HOW NOW! WHAT NEWS?

HATH HE ASKED FOR ME?

KNOW YOU NOT HE HAS?

HE HAS ALMOST SUPPED: WHY HAVE YOU LEFT THE CHAMBER?

WE WILL PROCEED NO FURTHUR IN THIS BUSINESS: HE HATH HONOURED ME OF LATE, AND I HAVE BOUGHT GOLDEN OPINIONS FROM ALL SORTS OF PEOPLE, WHICH WOULD BE WORN NOW IN THEIR NEWEST GLOSS, NOT CAST ASIDE SO SOON.

WAS THE HOPE DRUNK WHEREIN YOU DRESSED YOURSELF? HATH IT SLEPT SINCE? AND WAKES IT NOW, TO LOOK SO GREEN AND PALE AT WHAT IT DID SO FREELY? FROM THIS TIME SUCH I ACCOUNT THY LOVE. ART THOU AFEARED TO BE THE SAME IN THINE OWN ACT AND VALOUR AS THOU ART IN DESIRE? WOULDST THOU HAVE THAT WHICH THOU ESTEEM'ST THE ORNAMENT OF LIFE, AND LIVE A COWARD IN THINE OWN ESTEEM, LETTING 'I DARE NOT' WAIT UPON 'I WOULD', LIKE THE POOR CAT I' THE ADAGE?

WHAT BEAST WAS'T THEN THAT MADE YOU BREAK THIS ENTERPRISE TO ME? WHEN YOU DURST DO IT, THEN YOU WERE A MAN; AND, TO BE MORE THAN WHAT YOU WERE, YOU WOULD BE SO MUCH MORE THE MAN. NOR TIME NOR PLACE DID THEN ADHERE, AND YET YOU WOULD MAKE BOTH: THEY HAVE MADE THEMSELVES, AND THAT THEIR FITNESS NOW DOES UNMAKE YOU. I HAVE GIVEN SUCK, AND KNOW HOW TENDER 'TIS TO LOVE THE BABE THAT MILKS ME: I WOULD, WHILE IT WAS SMILING IN MY FACE, HAVE PLUCKED MY NIPPLE FROM HIS BONELESS GUMS AND DASHED THE BRAINS OUT, HAD I SO SWORN AS YOU HAVE DONE TO THIS.

PRITHEE, PEACE. I DARE DO ALL THAT MAY BECOME A MAN; WHO DARES DO MORE IS NONE.

IF WE SHOULD FAIL?

WE FAIL!

BUT SCREW YOUR COURAGE TO THE STICKING PLACE, AND WE'LL NOT FAIL. WHEN DUNCAN IS ASLEEP – WHERETO THE RATHER SHALL HIS DAY'S HARD JOURNEY SOUNDLY INVITE HIM – HIS TWO CHAMBERLAINS WILL I WITH WINE AND WASSAIL SO CONVINCE, THAT MEMORY, THE WARDER OF THE BRAIN, SHALL BE A FUME, AND THE RECEIPT OF

REASON A LIMBECK ONLY. WHEN IN SWINISH SLEEP THEIR DRENCHÈD NATURES LIES AS IN A DEATH, WHAT CANNOT YOU AND I PERFORM UPON THE UNGUARDED DUNCAN? WHAT NOT PUT UPON HIS SPONGY OFFICERS, WHO SHALL BEAR THE GUILT OF OUR GREAT QUELL?

BRING FORTH MEN-CHILDREN ONLY: FOR THY UNDAUNTED METTLE SHOULD COMPOSE NOTHING BUT MALES.

WILL IT NOT BE RECEIVED, WHEN WE HAVE MARKED WITH BLOOD THOSE SLEEPY TWO OF HIS OWN CHAMBER, AND USED THEIR VERY DAGGERS, THAT THEY HAVE DONE IT?

WHO DARES RECEIVE IT OTHER, AS WE SHALL MAKE OUR GRIEFS AND CLAMOUR ROAR UPON HIS DEATH?

I AM SETTLED; AND BEND UP EACH CORPORAL AGENT TO THIS TERRIBLE FEAT. AWAY, AND MOCK THE TIME WITH FAIREST SHOW: FALSE FACE MUST HIDE WHAT THE FALSE HEART DOTH KNOW.

IS THIS A DAGGER WHICH I SEE BEFORE ME, THE HANDLE TOWARD MY HAND?

COME, LET ME CLUTCH THEE:

I HAVE THEE NOT, AND YET I SEE THEE STILL!

ART THOU NOT, FATAL VISION, SENSIBLE TO FEELING AS TO SIGHT? OR ART THOU BUT A DAGGER OF THE MIND, A FALSE CREATION, PROCEEDING FROM THE HEAT-OPPRESSÈD BRAIN? I SEE THEE YET, IN FORM AS PALPABLE AS THIS WHICH NOW I DRAW. THOU MARSHALL'ST ME THE WAY THAT I WAS GOING, AND SUCH AN INSTRUMENT I WAS TO USE. MINE EYES ARE MADE FOOLS O'THE OTHER SENSES, OR ELSE WORTH ALL THE REST. —I SEE THEE STILL; AND ON THY BLADE AND DUDGEON, GOUTS OF BLOOD, WHICH WAS NOT SO BEFORE. THERE'S NO SUCH THING:

ACT II, SCENE II

THAT WHICH HATH MADE THEM DRUNK HATH MADE ME BOLD; WHAT HATH QUENCHED THEM HATH GIVEN ME FIRE. HARK! PEACE!

IT WAS THE OWL THAT SHRIEKED, THE FATAL BELLMAN, WHICH GIVES THE STERN'ST GOODNIGHT. HE IS ABOUT IT. THE DOORS ARE OPEN, AND THE SURFEITED GROOMS DO MOCK THEIR CHARGE WITH SNORES: I HAVE DRUGGED THEIR POSSETS, THAT DEATH AND NATURE DO CONTEND ABOUT THEM, WHETHER THEY LIVE OR DIE.

WHO'S THERE? WHAT, HO!

ALACK! I AM AFRAID THEY HAVE AWAKED AND 'TIS NOT DONE: THE ATTEMPT AND NOT THE DEED CONFOUNDS US. HARK! I LAID THEIR DAGGERS READY; HE COULD NOT MISS 'EM. HAD HE NOT RESEMBLED MY FATHER AS HE SLEPT, I HAD DONE'T.

MY HUSBAND!

I HAVE DONE THE DEED. DIDST THOU NOT HEAR A NOISE?

I HEARD THE OWL SCREAM AND THE CRICKETS CRY. DID YOU NOT SPEAK?

WHEN?

NOW.

AS I DESCENDED?

AY.

HARK! WHO LIES I' THE SECOND CHAMBER?

DONALBAIN.

THIS IS A SORRY SIGHT.

A FOOLISH THOUGHT, TO SAY A SORRY SIGHT.

THERE'S ONE DID LAUGH IN'S SLEEP, AND ONE CRIED 'MURDER!' THAT THEY DID WAKE EACH OTHER. I STOOD AND HEARD THEM. BUT THEY DID SAY THEIR PRAYERS, AND ADDRESSED THEM AGAIN TO SLEEP.

THERE ARE TWO LODGED TOGETHER.

ONE CRIED 'GOD BLESS US!' AND 'AMEN' THE OTHER, AS THEY HAD SEEN ME WITH THESE HANGMAN'S HANDS. LISTENING THEIR FEAR, I COULD NOT SAY 'AMEN', WHEN THEY DID SAY 'GOD BLESS US!'

CONSIDER IT NOT SO DEEPLY.

BUT WHEREFORE COULD I NOT PRONOUNCE 'AMEN'? I HAD MOST NEED OF BLESSING, AND 'AMEN' STUCK IN MY THROAT.

THESE DEEDS MUST NOT BE THOUGHT AFTER THESE WAYS; SO, IT WILL MAKE US MAD.

METHOUGHT I HEARD A VOICE CRY 'SLEEP NO MORE! MACBETH DOTH MURDER SLEEP,' —THE INNOCENT SLEEP, SLEEP THAT KNITS UP THE RAVELLED SLEAVE OF CARE, THE DEATH OF EACH DAY'S LIFE, SORE LABOUR'S BATH, BALM OF HURT MINDS, GREAT NATURE'S SECOND COURSE, CHIEF NOURISHER IN LIFE'S FEAST,—

WHAT DO YOU MEAN?

STILL IT CRIED, 'SLEEP NO MORE!' TO ALL THE HOUSE: 'GLAMIS HATH MURDERED SLEEP, AND THEREFORE CAWDOR SHALL SLEEP NO MORE: MACBETH SHALL SLEEP NO MORE!'

WHO WAS IT THAT THUS CRIED? WHY, WORTHY THANE, YOU DO UNBEND YOUR NOBLE STRENGTH, TO THINK SO BRAINSICKLY OF THINGS. GO, GET SOME WATER, AND WASH THIS FILTHY WITNESS FROM YOUR HAND. WHY DID YOU BRING THESE DAGGERS FROM THE PLACE? THEY MUST LIE THERE: GO, CARRY THEM, AND SMEAR THE SLEEPY GROOMS WITH BLOOD.

I'LL GO NO MORE: I AM AFRAID TO THINK WHAT I HAVE DONE; LOOK ON'T AGAIN I DARE NOT.

26

EXIT LADY MACBETH

INFIRM OF PURPOSE! GIVE ME THE DAGGERS. THE SLEEPING AND THE DEAD ARE BUT AS PICTURES. 'TIS THE EYE OF CHILDHOOD THAT FEARS A PAINTED DEVIL. IF HE DO BLEED, I'LL GILD THE FACES OF THE GROOMS WITHAL, FOR IT MUST SEEM THEIR GUILT.

WHENCE IS THAT KNOCKING? HOW IS'T WITH ME, WHEN EVERY NOISE APPALS ME? WHAT HANDS ARE HERE! HA! THEY PLUCK OUT MINE EYES! WILL ALL GREAT NEPTUNE'S OCEAN WASH THIS BLOOD CLEAN FROM MY HAND? NO, THIS MY HAND WILL RATHER THE MULTITUDINOUS SEAS INCARNADINE, MAKING THE GREEN ONE RED.

ENTER LADY MACBETH.

MY HANDS ARE OF YOUR COLOUR, BUT I SHAME TO WEAR A HEART SO WHITE.

I HEAR A KNOCKING AT THE SOUTH ENTRY. RETIRE WE TO OUR CHAMBER: A LITTLE WATER CLEARS US OF THIS DEED; HOW EASY IS IT THEN! YOUR CONSTANCY HATH LEFT YOU UNATTENDED.

HARK! MORE KNOCKING.

GET ON YOUR NIGHTGOWN, LEST OCCASION CALL US AND SHOW US TO BE WATCHERS. BE NOT LOST SO POORLY IN YOUR THOUGHTS.

TO KNOW MY DEED, T'WERE BEST NOT KNOW MYSELF.

WAKE DUNCAN WITH THY KNOCKING! I WOULD THOU COULDST!

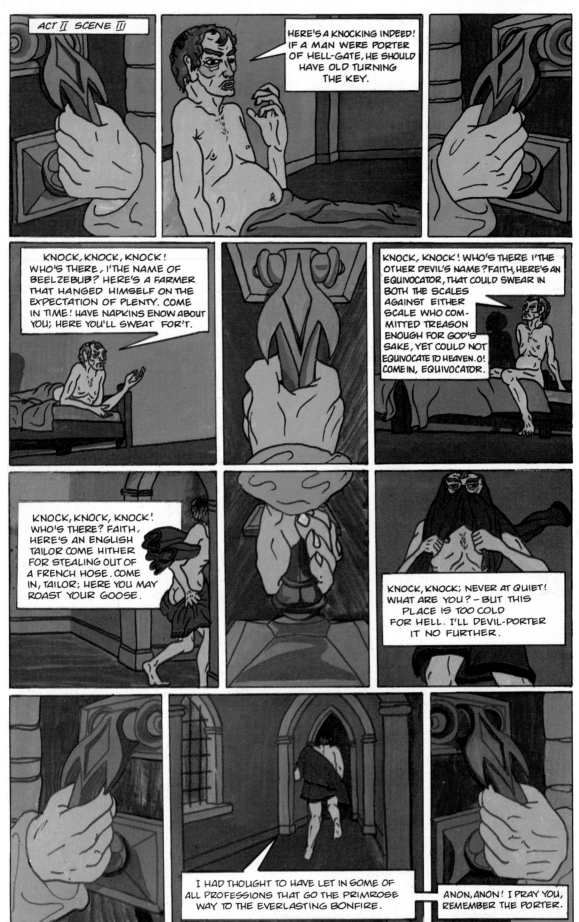

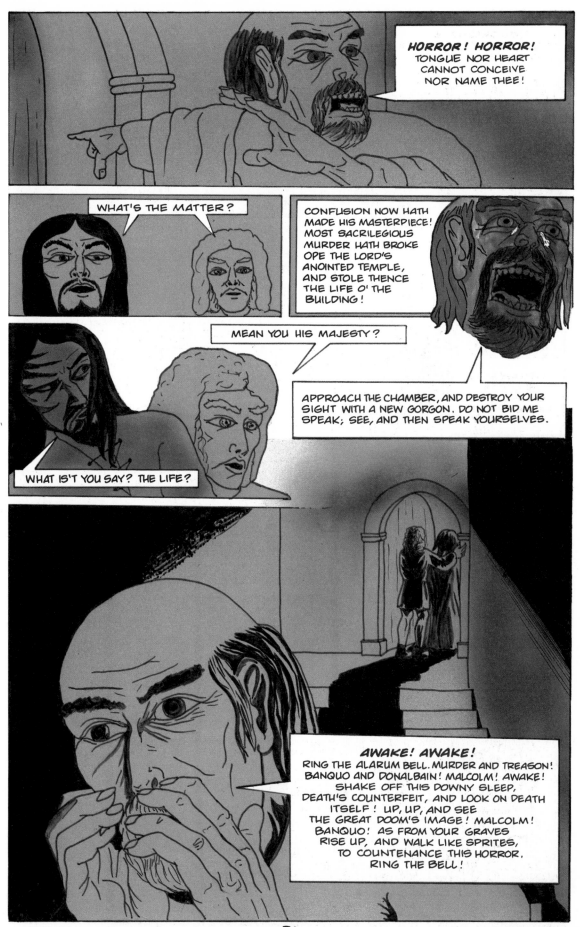

AND WHEN WE HAVE OUR NAKED FRAILTIES HID, THAT SUFFER IN EXPOSURE, LET US MEET AND QUESTION THIS MOST BLOODY PIECE OF WORK, TO KNOW IT FURTHER. FEARS AND SCRUPLES SHAKE US. IN THE GREAT HAND OF GOD I STAND, AND THENCE AGAINST THE UNDIVULGED PRETENCE I FIGHT OF TREASONOUS MALICE.

AND SO DO I.

SO ALL.

LET'S BRIEFLY PUT ON MANLY READINESS. AND MEET I'THE HALL TOGETHER.

WELL CONTENTED.

WHAT WILL YOU DO? LET'S NOT CONSORT WITH THEM. TO SHOW AN UNFELT SORROW IS AN OFFICE WHICH THE FALSE MAN DOES EASY. I'LL TO ENGLAND.

TO IRELAND, I; OUR SEPARATED FORTUNE SHALL KEEP US BOTH THE SAFER. WHERE WE ARE THERE'S DAGGERS IN MEN'S SMILES: THE NEAR IN BLOOD, THE NEARER BLOODY.

THIS MURDEROUS SHAFT THAT'S SHOT HATH NOT YET LIGHTED, AND OUR SAFEST WAY IS TO AVOID THE AIM. THEREFORE TO HORSE, AND LET US NOT BE DAINTY OF LEAVE-TAKING.

BUT SHIFT AWAY. THERE'S WARRANT IN THAT THEFT WHICH STEALS ITSELF WHEN THERE'S NO MERCY LEFT.

ENTER ROSS AND AN OLD MAN.

THREESCORE AND TEN I CAN REMEMBER WELL;
WITHIN THE VOLUME OF WHICH TIME
I HAVE SEEN HOURS DREADFUL AND THINGS
STRANGE, BUT THIS SORE NIGHT
HATH TRIFLED FORMER KNOWINGS.

'TIS UNNATURAL,
EVEN LIKE THE DEED THAT'S DONE.
ON TUESDAY LAST A FALCON, TOWERING IN
HER PRIDE OF PLACE, WAS BY A
MOUSING OWL HAWKED AT AND KILLED.

HA, GOOD FATHER,
THOU SEEST THE HEAVENS, AS TROUBLED
WITH MAN'S ACT,
THREATENS HIS BLOODY STAGE.
BY THE CLOCK 'TIS DAY, AND YET DARK NIGHT
STRANGLES THE TRAVELLING LAMP:
IS'T NIGHT'S PREDOMINANCE OR THE DAY'S
SHAME, THAT DARKNESS DOES THE FACE OF
EARTH ENTOMB, WHEN LIVING LIGHT SHOULD
KISS IT.

AND DUNCAN'S HORSES - A THING MOST
STRANGE AND CERTAIN - BEAUTEOUS AND
SWIFT, THE MINIONS OF THEIR RACE, TURNED
WILD IN NATURE, BROKE THEIR STALLS,
FLUNG OUT, CONTENDING 'GAINST OBEDIENCE,
AS THEY WOULD MAKE WAR WITH MANKIND.

'TIS SAID THEY EAT EACH OTHER.

THEY DID SO,
TO THE AMAZEMENT OF MINE EYES
THAT LOOKED UPON'T.
HERE COMES THE GOOD MACDUFF.
HOW GOES THE WORLD, SIR, NOW?

WHY, SEE YOU NOT?

35

TO BE THUS IS NOTHING, BUT TO BE SAFELY THUS.—
OUR FEARS IN BANQUO STICK DEEP.
AND IN HIS ROYALTY OF NATURE REIGNS
THAT WHICH WOULD BE FEARED.
'TIS MUCH HE DARES, AND, TO THAT
DAUNTLESS TEMPER OF HIS MIND, HE HATH
A WISDOM THAT DOTH GUIDE HIS VALOUR
TO ACT IN SAFETY.
THERE IS NONE BUT HE WHOSE BEING I DO
FEAR; AND UNDER HIM MY GENIUS IS
REBUKED, AS IT IS SAID MARK ANTHONY'S
WAS BY CAESAR. HE CHID THE SISTERS
WHEN FIRST THEY PUT THE NAME
OF KING UPON ME,
AND BADE THEM SPEAK TO HIM;
THEN, PROPHET-LIKE,
THEY HAILED HIM FATHER
TO A LINE OF KINGS. UPON
MY HEAD THEY PLACED
A FRUITLESS CROWN,
AND PUT A BARREN
SCEPTRE IN
MY GRIP.

THENCE TO BE WRENCHED WITH
AN UNLINEAL HAND, NO SON
OF MINE SUCCEEDING. IF IT
BE SO, FOR BANQUO'S
ISSUE HAVE I 'FILED MY MIND:
FOR THEM THE GRACIOUS
DUNCAN HAVE I MURDERED;
PUT RANCOURS IN THE VESSEL
OF MY PEACE, ONLY FOR THEM;
AND MINE ETERNAL JEWEL
GIVEN TO THE COMMON
ENEMY OF MAN,
TO MAKE THEM KINGS,
THE SEED OF BANQUO KINGS!
RATHER THAN SO,
COME FATE INTO THE LIST AND
CHAMPION ME TO
THE UTTERANCE!
WHO'S THERE?

NOW GO TO THE DOOR AND STAY THERE TILL WE CALL.

WAS IT NOT YESTERDAY WE SPOKE TOGETHER?

IT WAS, SO PLEASE
YOUR HIGHNESS.

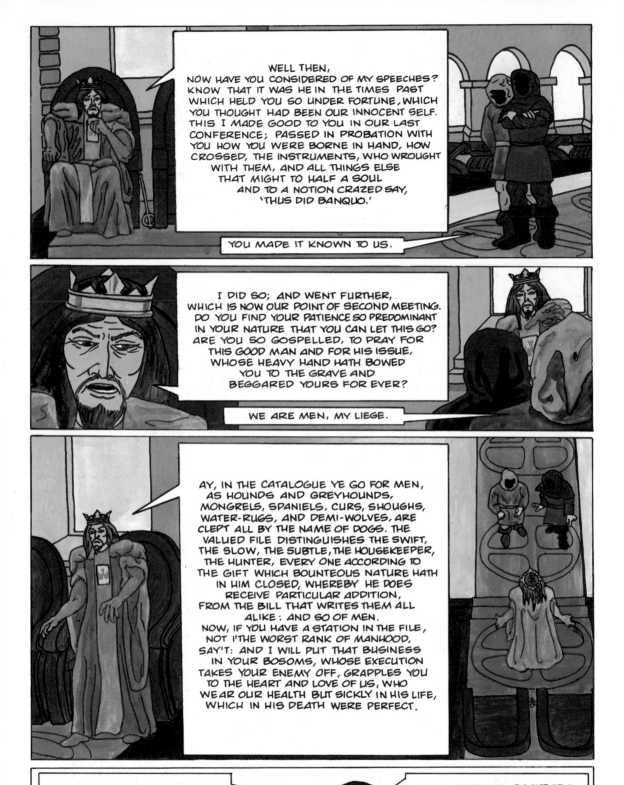

WELL THEN,
NOW HAVE YOU CONSIDERED OF MY SPEECHES?
KNOW THAT IT WAS HE IN THE TIMES PAST
WHICH HELD YOU SO UNDER FORTUNE, WHICH
YOU THOUGHT HAD BEEN OUR INNOCENT SELF.
THIS I MADE GOOD TO YOU IN OUR LAST
CONFERENCE; PASSED IN PROBATION WITH
YOU HOW YOU WERE BORNE IN HAND, HOW
CROSSED, THE INSTRUMENTS, WHO WROUGHT
WITH THEM, AND ALL THINGS ELSE
THAT MIGHT TO HALF A SOUL
AND TO A NOTION CRAZED SAY,
'THUS DID BANQUO.'

YOU MADE IT KNOWN TO US.

I DID SO; AND WENT FURTHER,
WHICH IS NOW OUR POINT OF SECOND MEETING.
DO YOU FIND YOUR PATIENCE SO PREDOMINANT
IN YOUR NATURE THAT YOU CAN LET THIS GO?
ARE YOU SO GOSPELLED, TO PRAY FOR
THIS GOOD MAN AND FOR HIS ISSUE,
WHOSE HEAVY HAND HATH BOWED
YOU TO THE GRAVE AND
BEGGARED YOURS FOR EVER?

WE ARE MEN, MY LIEGE.

AY, IN THE CATALOGUE YE GO FOR MEN,
AS HOUNDS AND GREYHOUNDS,
MONGRELS, SPANIELS, CURS, SHOUGHS,
WATER-RUGS, AND DEMI-WOLVES, ARE
CLEPT ALL BY THE NAME OF DOGS. THE
VALUED FILE DISTINGUISHES THE SWIFT,
THE SLOW, THE SUBTLE, THE HOUSEKEEPER,
THE HUNTER, EVERY ONE ACCORDING TO
THE GIFT WHICH BOUNTEOUS NATURE HATH
IN HIM CLOSED, WHEREBY HE DOES
RECEIVE PARTICULAR ADDITION,
FROM THE BILL THAT WRITES THEM ALL
ALIKE: AND SO OF MEN.
NOW, IF YOU HAVE A STATION IN THE FILE,
NOT I'THE WORST RANK OF MANHOOD,
SAY'T: AND I WILL PUT THAT BUSINESS
IN YOUR BOSOMS, WHOSE EXECUTION
TAKES YOUR ENEMY OFF, GRAPPLES YOU
TO THE HEART AND LOVE OF US, WHO
WEAR OUR HEALTH BUT SICKLY IN HIS LIFE,
WHICH IN HIS DEATH WERE PERFECT.

I AM ONE, MY LIEGE, WHOM THE
VILE BLOWS AND BUFFETS OF
THE WORLD HATH SO INCENSED
THAT I AM RECKLESS WHAT I DO
TO SPITE THE WORLD.

AND I ANOTHER, SO WEARY
WITH DISASTERS, TUGGED
WITH FORTUNE, THAT I WOULD
SET MY LIFE ON ANY CHANCE,
TO MEND IT OR BE RID ON'T.

ACT III SCENE II

IS BANQUO GONE FROM COURT?

AY, MADAM, BUT RETURNS AGAIN TONIGHT.

SAY TO THE KING I WOULD ATTEND HIS LEISURE FOR A FEW WORDS.

MADAM, I WILL.

NOUGHT'S HAD, ALL'S SPENT, WHERE OUR DESIRE IS GOT WITHOUT CONTENT. 'TIS SAFER TO BE THAT WHICH WE DESTROY THAN BY DESTRUCTION DWELL IN DOUBTFUL JOY.

HOW NOW, MY LORD! WHY DO YOU KEEP ALONE, OF SORRIEST FANCIES YOUR COMPANIONS MAKING, USING THOSE THOUGHTS WHICH SHOULD INDEED HAVE DIED WITH THEM THEY THINK ON? THINGS WITHOUT ALL REMEDY SHOULD BE WITHOUT REGARD: WHAT'S DONE IS DONE.

WE HAVE SCORCHED THE SNAKE, NOT KILLED IT: SHE'LL CLOSE AND BE HERSELF, WHILST OUR POOR MALICE REMAINS IN DANGER OF HER FORMER TOOTH. BUT LET THE FRAME OF THINGS DISJOINT, BOTH THE WORLDS SUFFER, ERE WE WILL EAT OUR MEAL IN FEAR, AND SLEEP IN THE AFFLICTION OF THESE TERRIBLE DREAMS THAT SHAKE US NIGHTLY: BETTER BE WITH THE DEAD, WHOM WE, TO GAIN OUR PEACE, HAVE SENT TO PEACE, THAN ON THE TORTURE OF THE MIND TO LIE IN RESTLESS ECSTASY. DUNCAN IS IN HIS GRAVE; AFTER LIFE'S FITFUL FEVER HE SLEEPS WELL; TREASON HAS DONE HIS WORST: NOR STEEL, NOR POISON, MALICE DOMESTIC, FOREIGN LEVY, NOTHING CAN TOUCH HIM FURTHER.

COME ON; GENTLE MY LORD, SLEEK O'ER YOUR RUGGED LOOKS; BE BRIGHT AND JOVIAL AMONG YOUR GUESTS TONIGHT.

SO SHALL I, LOVE, AND SO, I PRAY, BE YOU. LET YOUR REMEMBRANCE APPLY TO BANQUO;

PRESENT HIM EMINENCE,
BOTH WITH EYE AND TONGUE:
UNSAFE THE WHILE, THAT WE MUST LAVE
OUR HONOURS IN THESE FLATTERING STREAMS,
AND MAKE OUR FACES VIZARDS TO OUR HEARTS,
DISGUISING WHAT THEY ARE.

YOU MUST LEAVE THIS.

O! FULL OF SCORPIONS IS MY MIND, DEAR WIFE;
THOU KNOW'ST THAT BANQUO AND HIS FLEANCE LIVES.

BUT IN THEM NATURE'S COPY'S NOT ETERNE.

THERE'S COMFORT YET; THEY ARE ASSAILABLE.
THEN BE THOU JOCUND. ERE THE BAT HATH
FLOWN HIS CLOISTERED FLIGHT, ERE TO
BLACK HECATE'S SUMMONS THE SHARD-
BORNE BEETLE WITH HIS DROWSY HUMS
HATH RUNG NIGHT'S YAWNING PEAL, THERE
SHALL BE DONE A DEED OF DREADFUL NOTE.

WHAT'S TO BE DONE?

BE INNOCENT OF THE KNOWLEDGE,
DEAREST CHUCK, TILL THOU APPLAUD THE
DEED. COME, SEELING NIGHT,
SCARF UP THE TENDER EYE OF PITIFUL DAY,
AND WITH THY BLOODY AND INVISIBLE HAND
CANCEL AND TEAR TO PIECES THAT GREAT
BOND WHICH KEEPS ME PALE!
LIGHT THICKENS, AND THE CROW MAKES
WING TO THE ROOKY WOOD: GOOD THINGS
OF DAY BEGIN TO DROOP AND DROWSE,
WHILES NIGHT'S BLACK AGENTS TO THEIR
DO ROUSE. THOU MARVELL'ST AT MY WORDS:
BUT HOLD THEE STILL: THINGS BAD BEGUN
MAKE STRONG THEMSELVES BY ILL.
SO, PRITHEE, GO WITH ME.

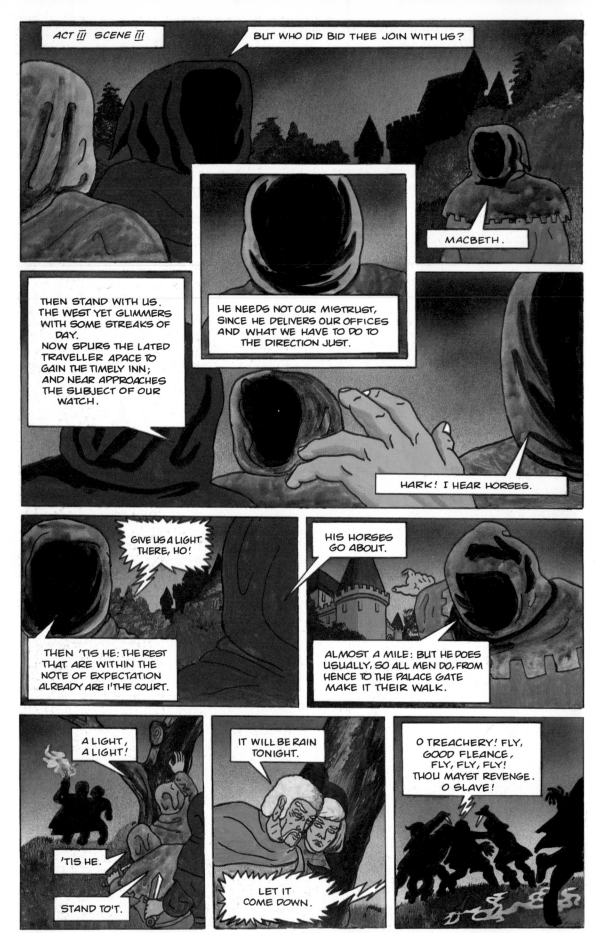

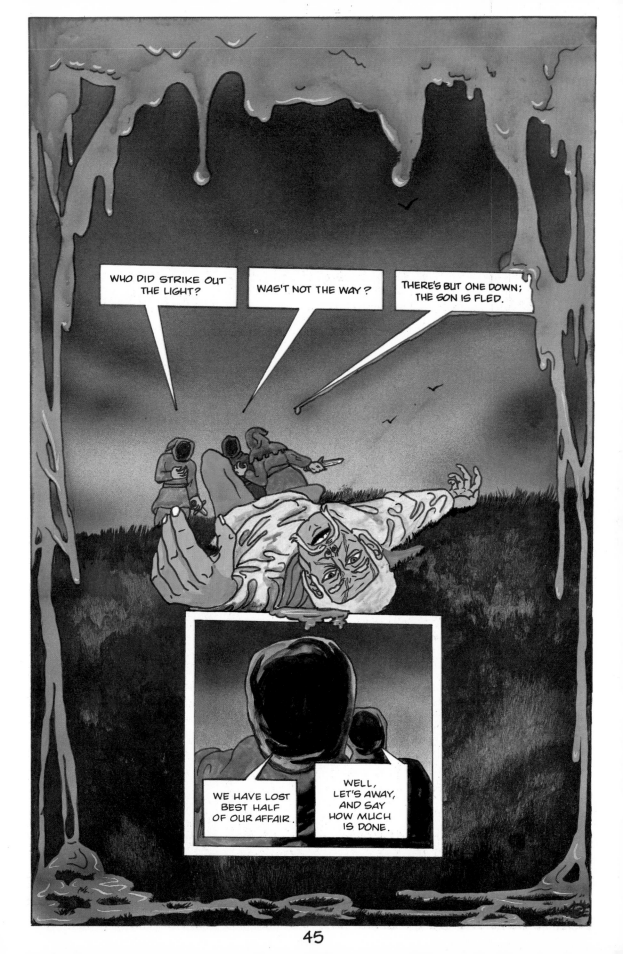

THOU ART THE BEST O' THE CUT-THROATS. YET HE'S GOOD THAT DID THE LIKE FOR FLEANCE. IF THOU DIDST IT, THOU ART THE NONPAREIL.

AY, MY GOOD LORD; SAFE IN A DITCH HE BIDES, WITH TWENTY TRENCHÈD GASHES ON HIS HEAD, THE LEAST A DEATH TO NATURE.

MOST ROYAL SIR — FLEANCE IS 'SCAPED.

THEN COMES MY FIT AGAIN: I HAD ELSE BEEN PERFECT; WHOLE AS THE MARBLE, FOUNDED AS THE ROCK, AS BROAD AND GENERAL AS THE CASING AIR: BUT NOW I AM CABINED, CRIBBED, CONFINED, BOUND IN TO SAUCY DOUBTS AND FEARS. — BUT BANQUO'S SAFE?

THANKS FOR THAT. THERE THE GROWN SERPENT LIES; THE WORM THAT'S FLED HATH NATURE THAT IN TIME WILL VENOM BREED, NO TEETH FOR THE PRESENT. GET THEE GONE. TOMORROW WE'LL HEAR OURSELVES AGAIN.

MY ROYAL LORD, YOU DO NOT GIVE THE CHEER. THE FEAST IS SOLD THAT IS NOT OFTEN VOUCHED, WHILE 'TIS A-MAKING, 'TIS GIVEN WITH WELCOME. TO FEED WERE BEST AT HOME; FROM THENCE, THE SAUCE TO MEAT IS CEREMONY: MEETING WERE BARE WITHOUT IT.

SWEET REMEMBRANCER! NOW GOOD DIGESTION WAIT ON APPETITE, AND HEALTH ON BOTH!

MAY'T PLEASE YOUR HIGHNESS SIT.

HERE HAD WE NOW OUR COUNTRY'S HONOUR ROOFED, WERE THE GRACED PERSON OF OUR BANQUO PRESENT; WHO MAY I RATHER CHALLENGE FOR UNKINDNESS THAN PITY FOR MISCHANCE.

HIS ABSENCE, SIR, LAYS BLAME UPON HIS PROMISE. PLEASE'T YOUR HIGHNESS TO GRACE US WITH YOUR ROYAL COMPANY.

48

O PROPER STUFF! THIS IS THE VERY PAINTING OF YOUR FEAR. THIS IS THE AIR-DRAWN DAGGER WHICH YOU SAID LED YOU TO DUNCAN. O, THESE FLAWS AND STARTS - IMPOSTORS TO TRUE FEAR - WOULD WELL BECOME A WOMAN'S STORY AT A WINTER'S FIRE, AUTHORIZED BY HER GRANDAM. SHAME ITSELF! WHY DO YOU MAKE SUCH FACES? WHEN ALL'S DONE YOU LOOK BUT ON A STOOL.

PRITHEE, SEE THERE! BEHOLD! LOOK! LO! HOW SAY YOU? WHY, WHAT CARE I IF THOU CANST NOD, SPEAK, TOO! IF CHARNEL-HOUSES AND OUR GRAVES MUST SEND THOSE THAT WE BURY BACK, OUR MONUMENTS SHALL BE THE MAWS OF KITES.

WHAT! QUITE UNMANNED IN FOLLY?

IF I STAND HERE, I SAW HIM.

FIE, FOR SHAME!

BLOOD HATH BEEN SHED ERE NOW, I'THE OLDEN TIME, ERE HUMANE STATUTE PURGED THE GENTLE WEAL; AY, AND SINCE TOO, MURDERS HAVE BEEN PERFORMED TOO TERRIBLE FOR THE EAR. THE TIMES HAS BEEN, THAT, WHEN THE BRAINS WERE OUT, THE MAN WOULD DIE, AND THERE AN END: BUT NOW THEY RISE AGAIN, WITH TWENTY MORTAL MURDERS ON THEIR CROWNS, AND PUSH US FROM OUR STOOLS. THIS IS MORE STRANGE THAN SUCH A MURDER IS.

MY WORTHY LORD, YOUR NOBLE FRIENDS DO LACK YOU.

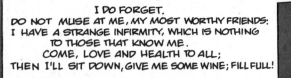
I DO FORGET.
DO NOT MUSE AT ME, MY MOST WORTHY FRIENDS:
I HAVE A STRANGE INFIRMITY, WHICH IS NOTHING
TO THOSE THAT KNOW ME.
COME, LOVE AND HEALTH TO ALL;
THEN I'LL SIT DOWN, GIVE ME SOME WINE; FILL FULL!

I DRINK TO THE GENERAL JOY O'THE WHOLE TABLE,
AND TO OUR DEAR FRIEND BANQUO, WHOM WE MISS;
WOULD HE WERE HERE!
TO ALL, AND HIM, WE THIRST,
AND ALL TO ALL!

OUR DUTIES AND THE PLEDGE!

AVAUNT! AND QUIT MY SIGHT!
LET THE EARTH HIDE THEE!
THY BONES ARE MARROWLESS, THY BLOOD IS
COLD; THOU HAST NO SPECULATION IN THOSE
EYES WHICH THOU DOST GLARE WITH.

THINK OF THIS, GOOD PEERS,
BUT AS A THING OF CUSTOM: 'TIS NO OTHER;
ONLY IT SPOILS THE PLEASURE OF THE TIME.

WHAT MAN DARE, I DARE.
APPROACH THOU LIKE THE RUGGED RUSSIAN
BEAR, THE ARMED RHINOCEROS, OR THE
HYRCAN TIGER; TAKE ANY SHAPE BUT THAT,
AND MY FIRM NERVES SHALL NEVER
TREMBLE. OR BE ALIVE AGAIN, AND DARE
ME TO THE DESERT WITH THY SWORD;
IF TREMBLING I INHABIT THEN, PROTEST
ME THE BABY OF A GIRL. HENCE,
HORRIBLE SHADOW!
UNREAL MOCKERY, HENCE!

WHY, SO; BEING GONE, I AM A MAN AGAIN. — PRAY YOU, SIT STILL.

YOU HAVE DISPLACED THE MIRTH, BROKE THE GOOD MEETING. WITH MOST ADMIRED DISORDER.

CAN SUCH THINGS BE, AND OVERCOME US LIKE A SUMMER'S CLOUD, WITHOUT OUR SPECIAL WONDER?

YOU MAKE ME STRANGE EVEN TO THE DISPOSITION THAT I OWE... WHEN NOW I THINK YOU CAN BEHOLD SUCH SIGHTS, AND KEEP THE NATURAL RUBY OF YOUR CHEEKS, WHEN MINE IS BLANCHED WITH FEAR.

WHAT SIGHTS, MY LORD?

I PRAY YOU, SPEAK NOT; HE GROWS WORSE AND WORSE; QUESTION ENRAGES HIM. AT ONCE, GOOD NIGHT. STAND NOT UPON THE ORDER OF YOUR GOING, BUT GO AT ONCE.

GOOD NIGHT; AND BETTER HEALTH ATTEND HIS MAJESTY!

A KIND GOOD NIGHT TO ALL!

WHY, HOW NOW, HECATE! YOU LOOK ANGERLY.

HAVE I NOT REASON, BELDAMS AS YOU ARE, SAUCY AND OVERBOLD? HOW DID YOU DARE TO TRADE AND TRAFFIC WITH MACBETH IN RIDDLES AND AFFAIRS OF DEATH; AND I, THE MISTRESS OF YOUR CHARMS, THE CLOSE CONTRIVER OF ALL HARMS, WAS NEVER CALLED TO BEAR MY PART, OR SHOW THE GLORY OF OUR ART? AND, WHICH IS WORSE, ALL YOU HAVE DONE HATH BEEN BUT FOR A WAYWARD SON, SPITEFUL AND WRATHFUL; WHO, AS OTHERS DO, LOVES FOR HIS OWN ENDS, NOT FOR YOU. BUT MAKE AMENDS NOW: GET YOU GONE, AND AT THE PIT OF ACHERON MEET ME IN THE MORNING: THITHER HE WILL COME TO KNOW HIS DESTINY. YOUR VESSELS AND YOUR SPELLS PROVIDE, YOUR CHARMS AND EVERYTHING BESIDE. I AM FOR THE AIR; THIS NIGHT I'LL SPEND UNTO A DISMAL AND A FATAL END: GREAT BUSINESS MUST BE WROUGHT ERE NOON: UPON THE CORNER OF THE MOON THERE HANGS A VAPOROUS DROP PROFOUND; I'LL CATCH IT ERE IT COME TO GROUND: AND THAT DISTILLED BY MAGIC SLEIGHTS SHALL RAISE SUCH ARTIFICIAL SPRITES AS BY THE STRENGTH OF THEIR ILLUSION SHALL DRAW HIM ON TO HIS CONFUSION. HE SHALL SPURN FATE, SCORN DEATH, AND BEAR HIS HOPES 'BOVE WISDOM, GRACE, AND FEAR: AND YOU ALL KNOW SECURITY IS MORTALS' CHIEFEST ENEMY.

HARK! I AM CALLED; MY LITTLE SPIRIT, SEE, SITS IN A FOGGY CLOUD, AND STAYS FOR ME.

COME, LET'S MAKE HASTE; SHE'LL SOON BE BACK AGAIN.

ENTER LENNOX AND ANOTHER LORD.

MY FORMER SPEECHES HAVE BUT HIT YOUR THOUGHTS, WHICH CAN INTERPRET FURTHER. ONLY I SAY THINGS HAVE BEEN STRANGELY BORNE.

THE GRACIOUS DUNCAN WAS PITIED OF MACBETH: MARRY, HE WAS DEAD! AND THE RIGHT VALIANT BANQUO WALKED TOO LATE; WHOM YOU MAY SAY, IF'T PLEASE YOU, FLEANCE KILLED FOR FLEANCE FLED.

MEN MUST NOT WALK TOO LATE WHO CANNOT WANT THE THOUGHT HOW MONSTROUS IT WAS FOR MALCOLM AND FOR DONALBAIN TO KILL THEIR GRACIOUS FATHER? DAMNÈD FACT! HOW IT DID GRIEVE MACBETH!

DID HE NOT STRAIGHT, IN PIOUS RAGE, THE TWO DELINQUENTS TEAR, THAT WERE THE SLAVES OF DRINK, AND THRALLS OF SLEEP? WAS NOT THAT NOBLY DONE? AY, AND WISELY TOO;

FOR 'TWOULD HAVE ANGERED ANY HEART ALIVE TO HEAR THE MEN DENY'T. SO THAT, I SAY, HE HAS BORNE ALL THINGS WELL: AND I DO THINK THAT, HAD HE DUNCAN'S SONS UNDER HIS KEY— AS, AN'T PLEASE HEAVEN, HE SHALL NOT— THEY SHOULD FIND WHAT 'TWERE TO KILL A FATHER; SO SHOULD FLEANCE.

BUT, PEACE! FOR FROM BROAD WORDS, AND 'CAUSE HE FAILED HIS PRESENCE AT THE TYRANT'S FEAST, I HEAR MACDUFF LIVES IN DISGRACE. SIR, CAN YOU TELL WHERE HE BESTOWS HIMSELF?

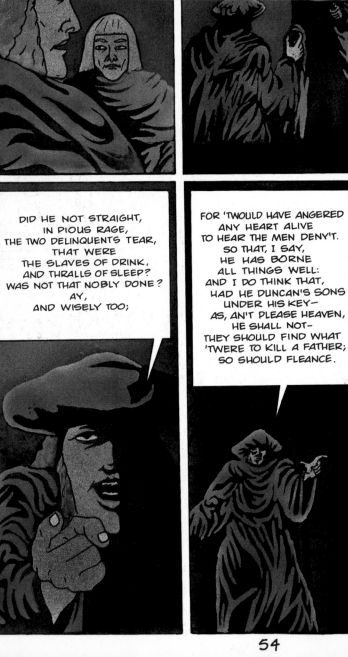

THE SON OF DUNCAN, FROM WHOM THIS TYRANT HOLDS THE DUE OF BIRTH, LIVES IN THE ENGLISH COURT, AND IS RECEIVED OF THE MOST PIOUS EDWARD WITH SUCH GRACE THAT THE MALEVOLENCE OF FORTUNE NOTHING TAKES FROM HIS HIGH RESPECT.

THITHER MACDUFF IS GONE TO PRAY THE HOLY KING, UPON HIS AID TO WAKE NORTHUMBERLAND AND WARLIKE SIWARD; THAT BY THE HELP OF THESE —WITH HIM ABOVE TO RATIFY THE WORK— WE MAY AGAIN GIVE TO OUR TABLES MEAT, SLEEP TO OUR NIGHTS,

FREE FROM OUR FEASTS AND BANQUETS BLOODY KNIVES, DO FAITHFUL HOMAGE AND RECEIVE FREE HONOURS; ALL WHICH WE PINE FOR NOW. AND THIS REPORT HATH SO EXASPERATE THE KING THAT HE PREPARES FOR SOME ATTEMPT OF WAR.

SENT HE TO MACDUFF?

HE DID: AND WITH AN ABSOLUTE, 'SIR, NOT I', THE CLOUDY MESSENGER TURNS ME HIS BACK, AND HUMS, AS WHO SHOULD SAY, 'YOU'LL RUE THE TIME THAT CLOGS ME WITH THIS ANSWER!'

AND THAT WELL MIGHT ADVISE HIM TO A CAUTION, TO HOLD WHAT DISTANCE HIS WISDOM CAN PROVIDE.

SOME HOLY ANGEL FLY TO THE COURT OF ENGLAND AND UNFOLD HIS MESSAGE ERE HE COME, THAT A SWIFT BLESSING MAY SOON RETURN TO THIS OUR SUFFERING COUNTRY UNDER A HAND ACCURSED!

I'LL SEND MY PRAYERS WITH HIM!

ACT IV SCENE I

THRICE THE BRINDED
CAT HATH MEWED.

THRICE, AND ONCE THE
HEDGE-PIG WHINED.

CRIES: 'TIS TIME, 'TIS TIME.

ROUND ABOUT THE CAULDRON GO; IN THE POISONED ENTRAILS THROW.
TOAD, THAT UNDER COLD STONE  DAYS AND NIGHTS HAS THIRTY-ONE.
SWELTERED VENOM SLEEPING GOT, BOIL THOU FIRST IN THE CHARMÈD POT.

DOUBLE, DOUBLE
TOIL AND TROUBLE;
FIRE BURN,
AND CAULDRON BUBBLE.

FILLET OF A
FENNY SNAKE, IN THE
CAULDRON BOIL AND BAKE;
EYE OF NEWT, AND TOE OF FROG,
WOOL OF BAT AND TONGUE OF DOG,
ADDER'S FORK AND BLIND-WORM'S
STING, LIZARD'S LEG AND HOWLET'S WING,
FOR A CHARM OF POWERFUL
TROUBLE, LIKE A HELL-BROTH BOIL AND BUBBLE.

DOUBLE, DOUBLE TOIL AND TROUBLE; FIRE BURN, AND CAULDRON BUBBLE.

SCALE OF DRAGON, TOOTH OF WOLF, WITCH'S MUMMY,
MAW AND GULF OF THE RAVINED SALT-SEA SHARK,
ROOT OF HEMLOCK DIGGED I'THE DARK, LIVER
OF BLASPHEMING JEW, GALL OF GOAT, AND
SLIPS OF YEW SLIVERED I'THE MOON'S
ECLIPSE, NOSE OF TURK, AND TARTAR'S
LIPS, FINGER OF BIRTH-STRANGLED
BABE, DITCH-DELIVERED BY A
DRAB, MAKE THE GRUEL
THICK AND SLAB: ADD
THERETO A TIGER'S
CHAUDRON, FOR THE
INGREDIENCE OF
OUR CAULDRON.

DOUBLE, DOUBLE
TOIL AND TROUBLE,
FIRE BURN, AND
CAULDRON BUBBLE.

COOL IT WITH A BABOON'S BLOOD, THEN THE CHARM IS FIRM AND GOOD.

O! WELL DONE! I COMMEND YOUR PAINS, AND EVERYONE SHALL SHARE I'THE GAINS: AND NOW ABOUT THE CAULDRON SING, LIKE ELVES AND FAIRIES IN A RING, ENCHANTING ALL THAT YOU PUT IN.

BY THE PRICKING OF MY THUMBS, SOMETHING WICKED THIS WAY COMES. OPEN, LOCKS, WHOEVER KNOCKS!

HOW NOW, YOU SECRET, BLACK, AND MIDNIGHT HAGS! WHAT IS'T YOU DO?

A DEED WITHOUT A NAME.

I CONJURE YOU, BY THAT WHICH YOU PROFESS— HOWE'ER YOU COME TO KNOW IT —ANSWER ME:

THOUGH YOU UNTIE THE WINDS AND LET THEM FIGHT AGAINST THE CHURCHES; THOUGH THE YESTY WAVES CONFOUND AND SWALLOW NAVIGATION UP; THOUGH BLADED CORN BE LODGED AND TREES BLOWN DOWN; THOUGH CASTLES TOPPLE ON THEIR WARDERS' HEADS;

THOUGH PALACES AND PYRAMIDS DO SLOPE THEIR HEADS TO THEIR FOUNDATIONS; THOUGH THE TREASURE OF NATURE'S GERMENS TUMBLE ALL TOGETHER, EVEN TILL DESTRUCTION SICKEN; ANSWER ME TO WHAT I ASK YOU.

SPEAK.

DEMAND.

WE'LL ANSWER.

SAY IF THOU'DST RATHER HEAR IT FROM OUR MOUTHS, OR FROM OUR MASTERS?

CALL 'EM: LET ME SEE 'EM.

POUR IN SOW'S BLOOD THAT HATH EATEN HER NINE FARROW; GREASE THAT'S SWEATEN FROM THE MURDERER'S GIBBET, THROW IN THE FLAME.

COME, HIGH OR LOW: THYSELF AND OFFICE DEFTLY SHOW.

TELL ME, THOU UNKNOWN POWER,—

HE KNOWS THY THOUGHT: HEAR HIS SPEECH, BUT SAY THOU NOUGHT.

MACBETH! MACBETH! MACBETH! BEWARE MACDUFF: BEWARE THE THANE OF FIFE! DISMISS ME. ENOUGH.

WHATE'ER THOU ART, FOR THY GOOD CAUTION THANKS. THOU HAST HARP'D MY FEAR ARIGHT. BUT ONE WORD MORE,—

HE WILL NOT BE COMMANDED, HERE'S ANOTHER, MORE POTENT THAN THE FIRST.

MACBETH! MACBETH! MACBETH!—

HAD I THREE EARS, I'D HEAR THEE.

BE BLOODY, BOLD, AND RESOLUTE; LAUGH TO SCORN THE POWER OF MAN, FOR NONE OF WOMAN BORN SHALL HARM MACBETH.

THEN LIVE, MACDUFF: WHAT NEED I FEAR OF THEE?

BUT YET I'LL MAKE ASSURANCE DOUBLE SURE, AND TAKE A BOND OF FATE: THOU SHALT NOT LIVE; THAT I MAY TELL PALE-HEARTED FEAR IT LIES, AND SLEEP IN SPITE OF THUNDER.

WHAT IS THIS, THAT RISES LIKE THE ISSUE OF A KING, AND WEARS UPON HIS BABY BROW THE ROUND AND TOP OF SOVEREIGNTY?

BE LION-METTLED, PROUD, AND TAKE NO CARE WHO CHAFES, WHO FRETS, OR WHERE CONSPIRERS ARE: MACBETH SHALL NEVER VANQUISHED BE, UNTIL GREAT BIRNAM WOOD TO HIGH DUNSINANE HILL SHALL COME AGAINST HIM.

LISTEN, BUT SPEAK NOT TO'T.

THAT WILL NEVER BE. WHO CAN IMPRESS THE FOREST, BID THE TREE UNFIX HIS EARTH-BOUND ROOT? SWEET BODEMENTS! GOOD! REBELLIOUS DEAD RISE NEVER TILL THE WOOD OF BIRNAM RISE, AND OUR HIGH-PLACED MACBETH SHALL LIVE THE LEASE OF NATURE, PAY HIS BREATH TO TIME AND MORTAL CUSTOM. YET MY HEART THROBS TO KNOW ONE THING: TELL ME, IF YOUR ART CAN TELL SO MUCH, SHALL BANQUO'S ISSUE EVER REIGN IN THIS KINGDOM?

SEEK TO KNOW NO MORE.

I WILL BE SATISFIED! DENY ME THIS, AND AN ETERNAL CURSE ON YOU! LET ME KNOW. WHY SINKS THAT CAULDRON? AND WHAT NOISE IS THIS?

SHOW! SHOW! SHOW!

SHOW HIS EYES, AND GRIEVE HIS HEART: COME LIKE SHADOWS, SO DEPART.

THOU ART TOO LIKE THE SPIRIT OF BANQUO: DOWN!
THY CROWN DOES SEAR MINE EYEBALLS.
AND THY HAIR, THOU OTHER GOLD-BOUND BROW, IS LIKE THE FIRST.
A THIRD IS LIKE THE FORMER. FILTHY HAGS! WHY DO YOU SHOW ME THIS? A FOURTH? START, EYES!
WHAT! WILL THE LINE STRETCH OUT TO THE CRACK OF DOOM? ANOTHER YET? A SEVENTH! I'LL SEE NO
MORE: AND YET THE EIGHTH APPEARS, WHO BEARS A GLASS WHICH SHOWS ME MANY MORE;
AND SOME I SEE THAT TWO-FOLD BALLS AND TREBLE SCEPTRES CARRY. HORRIBLE SIGHT!
NOW I SEE 'TIS TRUE, FOR THE BLOOD-BOLTERED BANQUO SMILES UPON ME,
AND POINTS AT THEM FOR HIS. WHAT! IS THIS SO?

AY, SIR, ALL THIS IS SO. BUT WHY STANDS MACBETH THUS AMAZÈDLY? COME, SISTERS, CHEER WE UP HIS SPRITES.

AND SHOW THE BEST OF OUR DELIGHTS. I'LL CHARM THE AIR TO GIVE A SOUND.

WHILE YOU PERFORM YOUR ANTIC ROUND, THAT THIS GREAT KING MAY KINDLY SAY OUR DUTIES DID HIS WELCOME PAY.

WHERE ARE THEY? GONE? LET THIS PERNICIOUS HOUR STAND AYE ACCURSÈD IN THE CALENDAR. COME IN, WITHOUT THERE!

WHAT'S YOUR GRACE'S WILL?

SAW YOU THE WEIRD SISTERS?

NO, MY LORD.

CAME THEY NOT BY YOU?

NO INDEED, MY LORD.

INFECTED BE THE AIR WHEREON THEY RIDE, AND DAMNED ALL THOSE THAT TRUST THEM! I DID HEAR THE GALLOPING OF HORSE. WHO WAS'T CAME BY?

'TIS TWO OR THREE, MY LORD, THAT BRING YOU WORD MACDUFF IS FLED TO ENGLAND.

FLED TO ENGLAND!

AY, MY GOOD LORD.

TIME, THOU ANTICIPAT'ST MY DREAD EXPLOITS: THE FLIGHTY PURPOSE NEVER IS O'ERTOOK UNLESS THE DEED GO WITH IT. FROM THIS MOMENT THE VERY FIRSTLINGS OF MY HEART SHALL BE THE FIRSTLINGS OF MY HAND. AND EVEN NOW, TO CROWN MY THOUGHTS WITH ACTS, BE IT THOUGHT AND DONE: THE CASTLE OF MACDUFF I WILL SURPRISE; SEIZE UPON FIFE, GIVE TO THE EDGE O'THE SWORD HIS WIFE, HIS BABES, AND ALL UNFORTUNATE SOULS THAT TRACE HIM IN HIS LINE. NO BOASTING LIKE A FOOL; THIS DEED I'LL DO BEFORE THIS PURPOSE COOL. BUT NO MORE SIGHTS! WHERE ARE THESE GENTLEMEN? COME, BRING ME WHERE THEY ARE.

ACT IV SCENE II

ENTER MACDUFF'S WIFE, HER SON, AND ROSS.

HE HAD NONE: HIS FLIGHT WAS MADNESS: WHEN OUR ACTIONS DO NOT, OUR FEARS DO MAKE US TRAITORS.

WHAT HAD HE DONE TO MAKE HIM FLY THE LAND?

YOU MUST HAVE PATIENCE, MADAM.

YOU KNOW NOT WHETHER IT WAS HIS WISDOM OR HIS FEAR.

WISDOM! TO LEAVE HIS WIFE, TO LEAVE HIS BABES, HIS MANSION AND HIS TITLES, IN A PLACE FROM WHENCE HIMSELF DOES FLY? HE LOVES US NOT; HE WANTS THE NATURAL TOUCH: FOR THE POOR WREN,

THE MOST DIMINUTIVE OF BIRDS, WILL FIGHT, HER YOUNG ONES IN THE NEST, AGAINST THE OWL. ALL IS THE FEAR AND NOTHING IS THE LOVE; AS LITTLE IS THE WISDOM, WHERE THE FLIGHT SO RUNS AGAINST ALL REASON.

MY DEAREST CUZ, I PRAY YOU, SCHOOL YOURSELF, BUT, FOR YOUR HUSBAND, HE IS NOBLE, WISE, JUDICIOUS, AND BEST KNOWS THE FITS O'THE SEASON. I DARE NOT SPEAK MUCH FURTHER: BUT CRUEL ARE THE TIMES, WHEN WE ARE TRAITORS AND DO NOT KNOW OURSELVES; WHEN WE HOLD RUMOUR FROM WHAT WE FEAR, YET KNOW NOT WHAT WE FEAR, BUT FLOAT UPON A WILD AND VIOLENT SEA EACH WAY AND MOVE. I TAKE MY LEAVE OF YOU: SHALL NOT BE LONG BUT I'LL BE HERE AGAIN. THINGS AT THE WORSE WILL CEASE, OR ELSE CLIMB UPWARD TO WHAT THEY WERE BEFORE. MY PRETTY COUSIN, BLESSING UPON YOU!

FATHERED HE IS, AND YET HE'S FATHERLESS.

I AM SO MUCH A FOOL, SHOULD I STAY LONGER IT WOULD BE MY DISGRACE, AND YOUR DISCOMFORT. I TAKE MY LEAVE AT ONCE.

SIRRAH, YOUR FATHER'S DEAD: AND WHAT WILL YOU DO NOW? HOW WILL YOU LIVE?

63

ACT IV SCENE III

ENTER MALCOLM AND MACDUFF.

LET US SEEK OUT SOME DESOLATE SHADE, AND THERE WEEP OUR SAD BOSOMS EMPTY.

LET US RATHER HOLD FAST THE MORTAL SWORD, AND LIKE GOOD MEN BESTRIDE OUR DOWNFALL BIRTHDOM. EACH NEW MORN NEW WIDOWS HOWL, NEW ORPHANS CRY, NEW SORROWS STRIKE HEAVEN ON THE FACE, THAT IT RESOUNDS AS IF IT FELT WITH SCOTLAND AND YELLED OUT LIKE SYLLABLE OF DOLOUR.

WHAT I BELIEVE, I'LL WAIL: WHAT KNOW, BELIEVE, AND WHAT I CAN REDRESS, AS I SHALL FIND THE TIME TO FRIEND, I WILL. WHAT YOU HAVE SPOKE, IT MAY BE SO PERCHANCE. THIS TYRANT, WHOSE SOLE NAME BLISTERS OUR TONGUES, WAS ONCE THOUGHT HONEST: YOU HAVE LOVED HIM WELL; HE HATH NOT TOUCHED YOU YET. I AM YOUNG; BUT SOMETHING YOU MAY DESERVE OF HIM, THROUGH ME: AND WISDOM TO OFFER UP A WEAK, POOR, INNOCENT LAMB TO APPEASE AN ANGRY GOD.

I AM NOT TREACHEROUS.

BUT MACBETH IS.

A GOOD AND VIRTUOUS NATURE MAY RECOIL IN AN IMPERIAL CHARGE. BUT I SHALL CRAVE YOUR PARDON; THAT WHICH YOU ARE MY THOUGHTS CANNOT TRANSPOSE: ANGELS ARE BRIGHT STILL THOUGH THE BRIGHTEST FELL: THOUGH ALL THINGS FOUL WOULD WEAR THE BROWS OF GRACE, YET GRACE MUST STILL LOOK SO.

I HAVE LOST MY HOPES.

PERCHANCE EVEN THERE WHERE I DID FIND MY DOUBTS. WHY IN THAT RAWNESS LEFT YOU WIFE AND CHILD— THOSE PRECIOUS MOTIVES, THOSE STRONG KNOTS OF LOVE— WITHOUT LEAVE-TAKING? I PRAY YOU, LET NOT MY JEALOUSIES BE YOUR DISHONOURS, BUT MINE OWN SAFETIES: YOU MAY BE RIGHTLY JUST, WHATEVER I SHALL THINK.

BLEED, BLEED,
POOR COUNTRY!
GREAT TYRANNY,
LAY THOU THY BASIS SURE,
FOR GOODNESS
DARE NOT CHECK THEE:
WEAR THOU THY WRONGS;
THE TITLE IS AFFEERED!
FARE THEE WELL, LORD:
I WOULD NOT BE THE VILLAIN
THAT THOU THINK'ST
FOR THE WHOLE SPACE
THAT'S IN THE TYRANT'S GRASP,
AND IN THE RICH EAST
TO BOOT.

BE NOT OFFENDED:
I SPEAK NOT AS IN ABSOLUTE FEAR OF YOU.
I THINK OUR COUNTRY SINKS BENEATH THE YOKE;
IT WEEPS, IT BLEEDS, AND EACH NEW DAY A GASH
IS ADDED TO HER WOUNDS. I THINK WITHAL,
THERE WOULD BE HANDS UPLIFTED IN MY RIGHT;
AND HERE FROM GRACIOUS ENGLAND HAVE I OFFER
OF GOODLY THOUSANDS. BUT FOR ALL THIS,
WHEN I SHALL TREAD UPON THE TYRANT'S HEAD,
OR WEAR IT UPON MY SWORD,
YET MY POOR COUNTRY
SHALL HAVE MORE VICES THAN IT HAD BEFORE,
MORE SUFFER,
AND MORE SUNDRY WAYS THAN EVER,
BY HIM THAT SHALL SUCCEED.

WHAT SHOULD HE BE?

IT IS MYSELF I MEAN; IN WHOM I KNOW
ALL THE PARTICULARS OF VICE SO GRAFTED
THAT, WHEN THEY SHALL BE OPENED,
BLACK MACBETH WILL SEEM AS PURE AS SNOW,
AND THE POOR STATE
ESTEEM HIM AS A LAMB, BEING COMPARED
WITH MY CONFINELESS HARMS.

NOT IN THE LEGIONS OF HORRID HELL CAN COME
A DEVIL MORE DAMNED IN EVILS TO TOP MACBETH.

I GRANT HIM BLOODY,
LUXURIOUS, AVARICIOUS, FALSE, DECEITFUL,
SUDDEN, MALICIOUS, SMACKING OF EVERY SIN
THAT HAS A NAME: BUT THERE'S NO BOTTOM, NONE,
IN MY VOLUPTUOUSNESS. YOUR WIVES,
YOUR DAUGHTERS, YOUR MATRONS, AND YOUR
MAIDS, COULD NOT FILL UP
THE CISTERN OF MY LUST; AND MY DESIRE
ALL CONTINENT IMPEDIMENTS WOULD O'ERBEAR
THAT DID OPPOSE MY WILL. BETTER MACBETH
THAN SUCH A ONE TO REIGN.

BOUNDLESS INTEMPERANCE
IN NATURE IS A TYRANNY; IT HATH BEEN
THE UNTIMELY EMPTYING OF THE HAPPY THRONE,
AND FALL OF MANY KINGS. BUT FEAR NOT YET
TO TAKE UPON YOU WHAT IS YOURS: YOU MAY
CONVEY YOUR PLEASURES IN A
SPACIOUS PLENTY AND YET SEEM
COLD, THE TIME YOU MAY SO HOODWINK.
WE HAVE WILLING DAMES ENOUGH;
THERE CANNOT BE THAT VULTURE
IN YOU TO DEVOUR SO MANY
AS WILL TO GREATNESS
DEDICATE THEMSELVES
FINDING IT SO INCLINED.

WITH THIS THERE GROWS
IN MY MOST ILL-COMPOSED AFFECTION
SUCH A STAUNCHLESS AVARICE THAT, WERE I KING,
I SHOULD CUT OFF THE NOBLES FOR THEIR LANDS,
DESIRE HIS JEWELS AND THIS OTHER'S HOUSE;
AND MY MORE-HAVING WOULD BE AS A
SAUCE TO MAKE ME HUNGER MORE, THAT I
SHOULD FORGE QUARRELS UNJUST
AGAINST THE GOOD AND LOYAL,
DESTROYING THEM FOR WEALTH.

THIS AVARICE STICKS DEEPER,
GROWS WITH MORE PERNICIOUS ROOT
THAN SUMMER-SEEMING LUST,
AND IT HATH BEEN THE SWORD
OF OUR SLAIN KINGS. YET DO NOT FEAR;
SCOTLAND HATH FOISONS
TO FILL UP YOUR WILL OF YOUR MERE OWN.
ALL THESE ARE PORTABLE,
WITH OTHER GRACES WEIGHED.

BUT I HAVE NONE.
THE KING-BECOMING GRACES,
AS JUSTICE, VERITY, TEMPERANCE, STABLENESS,
BOUNTY, PERSEVERANCE, MERCY, LOWLINESS,
DEVOTION, PATIENCE, COURAGE, FORTITUDE,
I HAVE NO RELISH OF THEM, BUT ABOUND
IN THE DIVISION OF EACH SEVERAL CRIME,
ACTING IT MANY WAYS.
NAY, HAD I POWER, I SHOULD POUR
THE SWEET MILK OF CONCORD INTO HELL,
UPROAR THE UNIVERSAL PEACE, CONFOUND
ALL UNITY ON EARTH.

O SCOTLAND, SCOTLAND!

IF SUCH A ONE BE FIT TO GOVERN,
SPEAK: I AM AS I HAVE SPOKEN.

FIT TO GOVERN!
NO, NOT TO LIVE! O NATION MISERABLE,
WITH AN UNTITLED TYRANT, BLOODY-SCEPTRED,
WHEN SHALT THOU SEE THY WHOLESOME DAYS AGAIN,
SINCE THAT THE TRUEST ISSUE OF THY THRONE
BY HIS OWN INTERDICTION STANDS ACCUSED,
AND DOES BLASPHEME HIS BREED?
THY ROYAL FATHER WAS A MOST SAINTED KING;
THE QUEEN THAT BORE THEE,
OFTENER UPON HER KNEES THAN ON HER FEET,
DIED EVERY DAY SHE LIVED. FARE THEE WELL!
THESE EVILS THOU REPEAT'ST UPON THYSELF
HATH BANISHED ME FROM SCOTLAND.
O MY BREAST,
THY HOPE ENDS HERE!

MACDUFF, THIS NOBLE PASSION,
CHILD OF INTEGRITY, HATH FROM MY SOUL
WIPED THE BLACK SCRUPLES
RECONCILED MY THOUGHTS
TO THY GOOD TRUTH AND HONOUR.
DEVILISH MACBETH BY MANY OF THESE TRAINS
HATH SOUGHT TO WIN ME INTO HIS POWER,
AND MODEST WISDOM PLUCKS ME
FROM OVER-CREDULOUS HASTE: BUT GOD ABOVE
DEAL BETWEEN THEE AND ME!
FOR EVEN NOW I PUT MYSELF TO THY
DIRECTION, AND UNSPEAK MY OWN DETRACTION,
HERE ABJURE THE TAINTS AND BLAMES
I LAID UPON MYSELF,
FOR STRANGERS TO MY NATURE.
I AM YET
UNKNOWN TO WOMAN, NEVER WAS FORSWORN,
SCARCELY HAVE COVETED WHAT WAS MINE OWN,
AT NO TIME BROKE MY FAITH,
WOULD NOT BETRAY THE DEVIL TO HIS FELLOW,
AND DELIGHT NO LESS IN TRUTH THAN LIFE.
MY FIRST FALSE SPEAKING
WAS THIS UPON MYSELF. WHAT I AM TRULY
IS THINE AND MY POOR COUNTRY'S
TO COMMAND; WHITHER INDEED,
BEFORE THY HERE-APPROACH,
OLD SIWARD WITH TEN THOUSAND
WARLIKE MEN, ALREADY AT A POINT,
WAS SETTING FORTH.
NOW WE'LL TOGETHER,
AND THE CHANCE OF GOODNESS
BE LIKE OUR WARRANTED QUARREL!
WHY ARE YOU SILENT?

SUCH WELCOME
AND UNWELCOME THINGS AT ONCE,
'TIS HARD TO RECONCILE.

WELL, MORE ANON. —
COMES THE KING FORTH, I PRAY YOU?

AY, SIR. THERE ARE A CREW OF WRETCHED SOULS THAT STAY HIS CURE. THEIR MALADY CONVINCES THE GREAT ASSAY OF ART; BUT, AT HIS TOUCH, SUCH SANCTITY HATH HEAVEN GIVEN HIS HAND, THEY PRESENTLY AMEND.

I THANK YOU, DOCTOR.

WHAT'S THE DISEASE HE MEANS?

'TIS CALLED THE EVIL: A MOST MIRACULOUS WORK IN THIS GOOD KING, WHICH OFTEN, SINCE MY HERE-REMAIN IN ENGLAND, I HAVE SEEN HIM DO. HOW HE SOLICITS HEAVEN HIMSELF BEST KNOWS: BUT STRANGELY-VISITED PEOPLE, ALL SWOLLEN AND ULCEROUS, PITIFUL TO THE EYE, THE MERE DESPAIR OF SURGERY, HE CURES; HANGING A GOLDEN STAMP ABOUT THEIR NECKS, PUT ON WITH HOLY PRAYERS; AND 'TIS SPOKEN, TO THE SUCCEEDING ROYALTY HE LEAVES THE HEALING BENEDICTION. WITH THIS STRANGE VIRTUE HE HATH A HEAVENLY GIFT OF PROPHECY, AND SUNDRY BLESSINGS HANG ABOUT HIS THRONE THAT SPEAK HIM FULL OF GRACE.

SEE, WHO COMES HERE?

MY COUNTRYMAN; BUT YET I KNOW HIM NOT.

MY EVER GENTLE COUSIN, WELCOME HITHER.

I KNOW HIM NOW. GOOD GOD, BETIMES REMOVE THE MEANS THAT MAKES US STRANGERS!

70

SIR, AMEN.

STANDS SCOTLAND WHERE IT DID?

ALAS, POOR COUNTRY, ALMOST AFRAID TO KNOW ITSELF! IT CANNOT BE CALLED OUR MOTHER, BUT OUR GRAVE; WHERE NOTHING, BUT WHO KNOWS NOTHING, IS ONCE SEEN TO SMILE; WHERE SIGHS AND GROANS AND SHRIEKS THAT RENT THE AIR ARE MADE, NOT MARKED; WHERE VIOLENT SORROW SEEMS A MODERN ECSTASY. THE DEAD MAN'S KNELL IS THERE SCARCE ASKED FOR WHO, AND GOOD MEN'S LIVES EXPIRE BEFORE THE FLOWERS IN THEIR CAPS, DYING OR ERE THEY SICKEN.

O, RELATION TOO NICE, AND YET TOO TRUE!

WHAT'S THE NEWEST GRIEF?

THAT OF AN HOUR'S AGE DOTH HISS THE SPEAKER; EACH MINUTE TEEMS A NEW ONE.

HOW DOES MY WIFE?

WHY, WELL.

AND ALL MY CHILDREN?

WELL, TOO.

THE TYRANT HAS NOT BATTERED AT THEIR PEACE?

NO, THEY WERE WELL AT PEACE WHEN I DID LEAVE 'EM.

BE NOT A NIGGARD OF YOUR SPEECH: HOW GOES'T?

WHEN I CAME HITHER TO TRANSPORT THE TIDINGS WHICH I HAVE HEAVILY BORNE, THERE RAN A RUMOUR OF MANY WORTHY FELLOWS THAT WERE OUT; WHICH WAS TO MY BELIEF WITNESSED THE RATHER FOR THAT I SAW THE TYRANT'S POWER AFOOT. NOW IS THE TIME OF HELP. YOUR EYE IN SCOTLAND WOULD CREATE SOLDIERS, MAKE OUR WOMEN FIGHT, TO DOFF THEIR DIRE DISTRESSES.

BE'T THEIR COMFORT, WE ARE COMING THITHER. GRACIOUS ENGLAND HATH LENT US GOOD SIWARD AND TEN THOUSAND MEN; AN OLDER AND BETTER SOLDIER NONE THAT CHRISTENDOM GIVES OUT.

WOULD I COULD ANSWER THIS COMFORT WITH THE LIKE! BUT I HAVE WORDS THAT WOULD BE HOWLED OUT IN THE DESERT AIR, WHERE HEARING SHOULD NOT LATCH THEM.

WHAT CONCERN THEY? THE GENERAL CAUSE? OR IS IT A FEE-GRIEF DUE TO SOME SINGLE BREAST?

NO MIND THAT'S HONEST BUT IN IT SHARES SOME WOE, THOUGH THE MAIN PART PERTAINS TO YOU ALONE.

LET NOT YOUR EARS DESPISE MY TONGUE FOR EVER, WHICH SHALL POSSESS THEM WITH THE HEAVIEST SOUND THAT EVER YET THEY HEARD.

IF IT BE MINE, KEEP IT NOT FROM ME; QUICKLY LET ME HAVE IT.

HUMH! I GUESS AT IT.

YOUR CASTLE IS SURPRISED; YOUR WIFE AND BABES SAVAGELY SLAUGHTERED. TO RELATE THE MANNER, WERE, ON THE QUARRY OF THESE MURDERED DEER, TO ADD THE DEATH OF YOU.

MERCIFUL HEAVEN!

WHAT, MAN! NE'ER PULL YOUR HAT UPON YOUR BROWS. GIVE SORROW WORDS: THE GRIEF THAT DOES NOT SPEAK WHISPERS THE O'ER-FRAUGHT HEART AND BIDS IT BREAK.

MY CHILDREN TOO?

WIFE, CHILDREN, SERVANTS, ALL THAT COULD BE FOUND.

AND I MUST BE FROM THENCE! MY WIFE KILLED TOO?

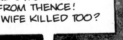

BE COMFORTED: LET'S MAKE US MED'CINES OF OUR GREAT REVENGE, TO CURE THIS DEADLY GRIEF.

I HAVE SAID.

HE HAS NO CHILDREN.
ALL MY PRETTY ONES? DID YOU SAY ALL?
O HELL-KITE! ALL?
WHAT, ALL MY PRETTY CHICKENS AND THEIR
DAM AT ONE FELL SWOOP?

DISPUTE IT LIKE A MAN.

I SHALL DO SO;
BUT I MUST ALSO FEEL IT AS A MAN.
I CANNOT BUT REMEMBER SUCH THINGS WERE,
THAT WERE MOST PRECIOUS TO ME.
DID HEAVEN LOOK ON AND WOULD NOT TAKE
THEIR PART? SINFUL MACDUFF,
THEY WERE ALL STRUCK FOR THEE! NAUGHT
THAT I AM, NOT FOR THEIR OWN DEMERITS,
BUT FOR MINE, FELL SLAUGHTER ON THEIR SOULS,
HEAVEN REST THEM NOW.

BE THIS THE WHETSTONE OF YOUR SWORD:
LET GRIEF CONVERT TO ANGER;
BLUNT NOT THE HEART, ENRAGE IT.

O, I COULD PLAY THE WOMAN WITH MINE EYES,
AND BRAGGART WITH MY TONGUE.
BUT, GENTLE HEAVENS, CUT SHORT ALL
INTERMISSION; FRONT TO FRONT BRING
THOU THIS FIEND OF SCOTLAND AND MYSELF;
WITHIN MY SWORD'S LENGTH SET HIM;
IF HE 'SCAPE, HEAVEN FORGIVE HIM TOO!

THIS TUNE GOES MANLY.
COME, GO WE TO THE KING; OUR POWER IS READY;
OUR LACK IS NOTHING BUT OUR LEAVE. MACBETH
IS RIPE FOR SHAKING, AND THE POWERS ABOVE
PUT ON THEIR INSTRUMENTS.
RECEIVE WHAT CHEER YOU MAY:
THE NIGHT IS LONG THAT NEVER FINDS THE DAY.

ACT V SCENE V

HANG OUT OUR BANNERS ON THE OUTWARD WALLS;
THE CRY IS STILL, 'THEY COME':
OUR CASTLE'S STRENGTH WILL LAUGH A SIEGE
TO SCORN: HERE LET THEM LIE
TILL FAMINE AND THE AGUE EAT THEM UP.
WERE THEY NOT FORCED WITH THOSE
THAT SHOULD BE OURS, WE MIGHT HAVE
MET THEM DAREFUL, BEARD TO BEARD,
AND BEAT THEM BACKWARD HOME.

WHAT IS THAT NOISE?

I HAVE ALMOST FORGOT THE TASTE OF FEARS.
THE TIME HAS BEEN MY SENSES WOULD
HAVE COOLED TO HEAR A NIGHT-SHRIEK,
AND MY FELL OF HAIR WOULD AT A
DISMAL TREATISE ROUSE AND STIR AS
LIFE WERE IN'T. I HAVE SUPPED FULL WITH
HORRORS;
DIRENESS, FAMILIAR TO MY SLAUGHTEROUS THOUGHTS,
CANNOT ONCE START ME.
WHEREFORE WAS THAT CRY?

IT IS THE CRY OF WOMEN,
MY GOOD LORD.

THE QUEEN, MY LORD, IS DEAD.

SHE SHOULD HAVE DIED HEREAFTER;
THERE WOULD HAVE BEEN A TIME
FOR SUCH A WORD. TOMORROW, AND TOMORROW,
AND TOMORROW, CREEPS IN THIS PETTY PACE
FROM DAY TO DAY,
TO THE LAST SYLLABLE OF RECORDED TIME;
AND ALL OUR YESTERDAYS HAVE LIGHTED FOOLS
THE WAY TO DUSTY DEATH.
OUT, OUT, BRIEF CANDLE!
LIFE'S BUT A WALKING SHADOW, A POOR PLAYER
THAT STRUTS AND FRETS HIS HOUR UPON THE STAGE,
AND THEN IS HEARD NO MORE. IT IS A TALE
TOLD BY AN IDIOT, FULL OF SOUND AND FURY,
SIGNIFYING NOTHING.

THOU COM'ST
TO USE THY TONGUE;
THY STORY QUICKLY!

GRACIOUS MY LORD,
I SHOULD REPORT THAT WHICH I SAY I SAW,
BUT KNOW NOT HOW TO DO IT.

AS I DID STAND MY WATCH UPON THE HILL,
I LOOKED TOWARD BIRNHAM, AND ANON METHOUGHT
THE WOOD BEGAN TO MOVE.

WELL, SAY, SIR.

LIAR AND SLAVE!

LET ME ENDURE YOUR WRATH IF'T BE NOT SO:
WITHIN THIS THREE MILE MAY YOU SEE IT COMING.
I SAY, A MOVING GROVE.

IF THOU SPEAK'ST FALSE,
UPON THE NEXT TREE SHALL THOU HANG ALIVE,
TILL FAMINE CLING THEE.

IF THY SPEECH BE SOOTH,
I CARE NOT IF THOU DOST FOR ME AS MUCH.
I PULL IN RESOLUTION, AND BEGIN TO DOUBT
THE EQUIVOCATION OF THE FIEND
THAT LIES LIKE TRUTH: 'FEAR NOT, TILL
BIRNAM WOOD DO COME TO DUNSINANE'—
AND NOW A WOOD COMES TOWARD DUNSINANE.
ARM, ARM, AND OUT!
IF THIS WHICH HE AVOUCHES DOES APPEAR,
THERE IS NOR FLYING HENCE, NOR TARRYING HERE.
I 'GIN TO BE AWEARY OF THE SUN,
AND WISH THE ESTATE
O'THE WORLD WERE NOW UNDONE.
RING THE ALARUM BELL! BLOW, WIND! COME, WRACK!
AT LEAST WE'LL DIE WITH HARNESS ON OUR BACK!

83

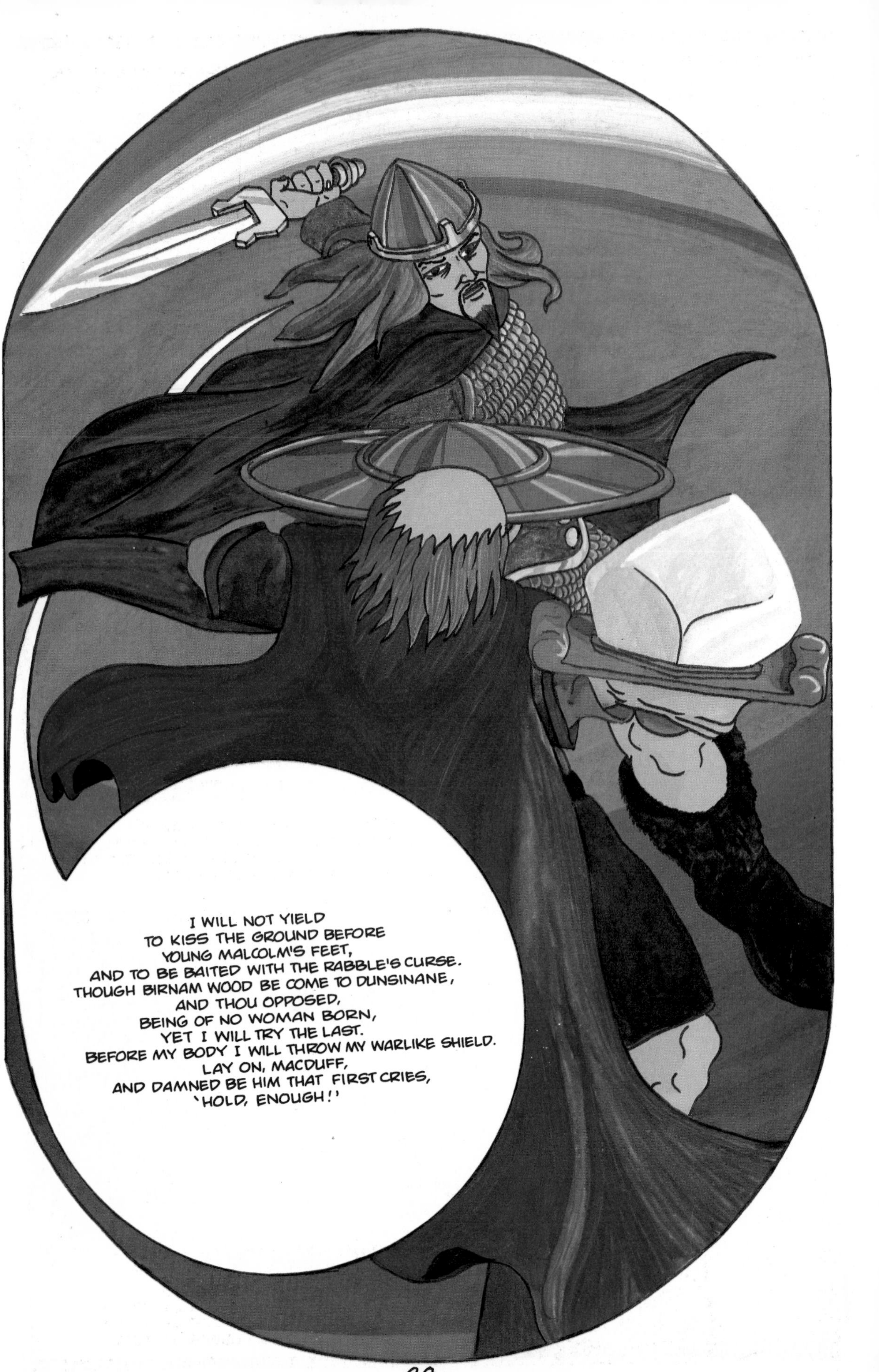

I WILL NOT YIELD
TO KISS THE GROUND BEFORE
YOUNG MALCOLM'S FEET,
AND TO BE BAITED WITH THE RABBLE'S CURSE.
THOUGH BIRNAM WOOD BE COME TO DUNSINANE,
AND THOU OPPOSED,
BEING OF NO WOMAN BORN,
YET I WILL TRY THE LAST.
BEFORE MY BODY I WILL THROW MY WARLIKE SHIELD.
LAY ON, MACDUFF,
AND DAMNED BE HIM THAT FIRST CRIES,
'HOLD, ENOUGH!'

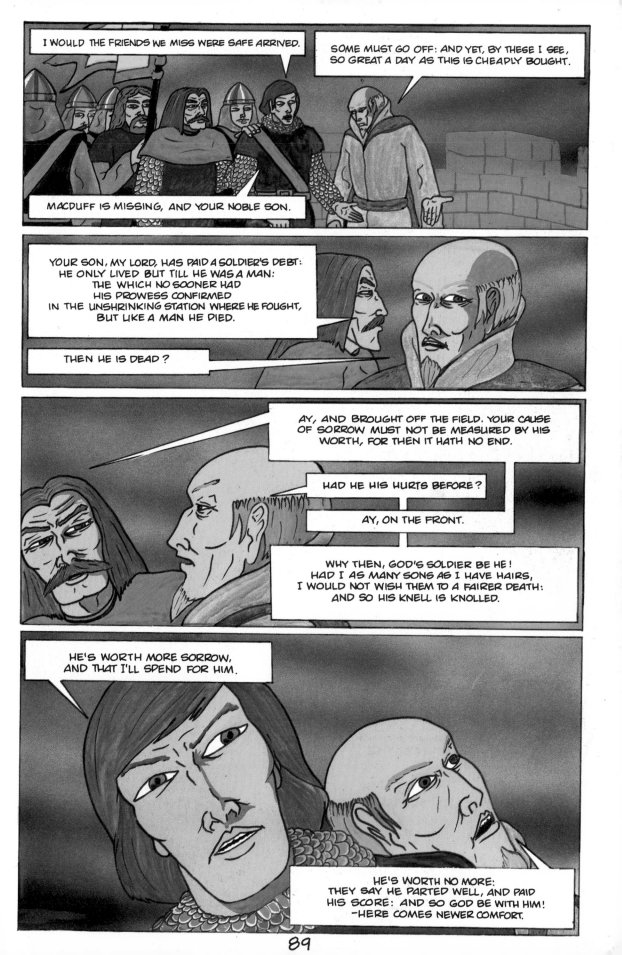

I WOULD THE FRIENDS WE MISS WERE SAFE ARRIVED.

SOME MUST GO OFF: AND YET, BY THESE I SEE, SO GREAT A DAY AS THIS IS CHEAPLY BOUGHT.

MACDUFF IS MISSING, AND YOUR NOBLE SON.

YOUR SON, MY LORD, HAS PAID A SOLDIER'S DEBT:
HE ONLY LIVED BUT TILL HE WAS A MAN:
THE WHICH NO SOONER HAD
HIS PROWESS CONFIRMED
IN THE UNSHRINKING STATION WHERE HE FOUGHT,
BUT LIKE A MAN HE DIED.

THEN HE IS DEAD?

AY, AND BROUGHT OFF THE FIELD. YOUR CAUSE OF SORROW MUST NOT BE MEASURED BY HIS WORTH, FOR THEN IT HATH NO END.

HAD HE HIS HURTS BEFORE?

AY, ON THE FRONT.

WHY THEN, GOD'S SOLDIER BE HE!
HAD I AS MANY SONS AS I HAVE HAIRS,
I WOULD NOT WISH THEM TO A FAIRER DEATH:
AND SO HIS KNELL IS KNOLLED.

HE'S WORTH MORE SORROW,
AND THAT I'LL SPEND FOR HIM.

HE'S WORTH NO MORE:
THEY SAY HE PARTED WELL, AND PAID
HIS SCORE: AND SO GOD BE WITH HIM!
—HERE COMES NEWER COMFORT.

HAIL, KING OF SCOTLAND!

WE SHALL NOT SPEND A LARGE EXPENSE
OF TIME BEFORE WE RECKON WITH
YOUR SEVERAL LOVES, AND MAKE US EVEN
WITH YOU.
MY THANES AND KINSMEN,
HENCEFORTH BE EARLS, THE FIRST THAT
EVER SCOTLAND IN SUCH AN HONOUR NAMED.
WHAT'S MORE TO DO, WHICH WOULD BE
PLANTED NEWLY WITH THE TIME, AS
CALLING HOME OUR EXILED FRIENDS ABROAD
THAT FLED THE SNARES OF WATCHFUL TYRANNY;
PRODUCING FORTH THE CRUEL MINISTERS OF
THIS DEAD BUTCHER AND HIS FIEND-LIKE QUEEN,
WHO, AS 'TIS THOUGHT,
BY SELF AND VIOLENT HANDS
TOOK OFF HER LIFE: THIS AND WHAT NEEDFUL ELSE
THAT CALLS UPON US, BY THE GRACE OF GRACE
WE WILL PERFORM IN MEASURE, TIME, AND PLACE.
SO, THANKS TO ALL AT ONCE AND TO EACH ONE,
WHOM WE INVITE TO SEE US
CROWNED AT SCONE.